CALVIN AND CALVINISM
Sources of Democracy?

PROBLEMS IN EUROPEAN CIVILIZATION

CALVIN AND CALVINISM

Sources of Democracy?

EDITED WITH AN INTRODUCTION BY

Robert M. Kingdon

THE UNIVERSITY OF WISCONSIN

and

Robert D. Linder

KANSAS STATE UNIVERSITY

D. C. HEATH AND COMPANY

Lexington, Massachusetts

Printed in the United States of America

Library of Congress Number: 79-134172

CONTENTS

INTRODUCTION

EVERY citizen active in the world today needs to have some understanding of the meaning of the term "democracy." It describes one of the most important and attractive options available to the many people of this world who at some time may be compelled to make decisions about the form of government under which they wish to live. Yet it is obvious that democracy means different things to different people. One has only to consider the different meanings of the term as used at this time in the United States by leaders of the Democratic Party and by members of the Students for a Democratic Society. This makes it all the more important for citizens to try to give some specific meaning to the term in order to prevent it from becoming an empty slogan. In the attempt to reach an understanding of what democracy should mean to citizens now, one may look to history for guidance. For democracy as we know it now, both as a concept and as a form of government, has had a long and varied career.

In seeking the historic roots of democracy, many historians have paused to examine the movement of Calvinism because of the rather striking correlation, both in time and in place, between the spread of Calvinist Protestantism and the rise of democracy. In the sixteenth century, Calvinist Protestantism spread rapidly from its headquarters in the Swiss city-state of Geneva to other parts of Switzerland, much of France, the Low Countries, England, and Scotland. In the seventeenth and eighteenth centuries, democracy won its first and strongest support in many of these same countries and in some of their dependencies, notably the English colonies in America. Within each of these countries, the democratic ideal often won its staunchest adherents from the very elements of the population which earlier had adopted Calvinism. A possible explanation of this correlation is that Calvinism in some way conditioned or perhaps even caused people to accept democracy. It is the purpose of this volume to assist in examining the validity of that possible explanation.

A historian may use a number of methods to investigate this kind of connection. Many of them have been tried by historians exploring the relationship between Calvinism and democracy. Often a single historian has combined several methods, even in the same work. For purposes of analysis and evaluation, however, it is helpful to separate these methods and to reduce them to a rather schematic framework. That is the aim of this introduction.

* * *

One obvious approach is to focus on the figure of Calvin himself. This method appeals especially to historians who believe that great men have an important influence on history. It also is attractive to historians who are themselves in some way associated with the Calvinist tradition, and to whom Calvin's teachings and example can still be of some normative value. It may even appeal to historians who are trying to escape from a Calvinist tradition and who are striving to free themselves of some of its pervasiveness in their own experience.

Explanations of the connections between Calvinism and democracy which center on Calvin can be made quite plausible. There is no denying that he had a charismatic personality and a powerful, synthetic mind which had a profound influence on the movement during its formative years. It is also certain that Calvin's followers treasured and used his writings for generations after his death. One might employ four clearly different ways to examine Calvin's connection with democracy.

The first and most obvious method is to study what Calvin said directly about politics. Calvin was not, to be sure, a political theorist, and he did not publish any treatises on politics. His voluminous publications were all on religious topics, primarily either works of systematic theology or commentaries on specific books of the Bible. The most important was his *Institutes of the Christian Religion,* which he kept revising and expanding throughout his life, and which became the most influential single summary of theology produced by the Protestant Reformation. A careful search of Calvin's religious works, however, does bring to light a number of passages in which he comments on political problems. They have been studied with great care by a number of extremely able modern scholars, including several whose arguments are presented in this volume. M. Marc-Edouard Chenevière and Professor John T. McNeill have probably used this method most intensively. The attentive reader will notice that a significant number of the scholars whose excerpted works are included in this volume comment on the same key passages from Calvin. But he also will quickly discover that they have different theories about the meaning of these passages. While some believe these passages show that Calvin favored democracy, others believe they reveal he favored aristocracy or mixed government, and still others believe they demonstrate he had no preferences for any one form of government.

Any attempt to explain why these theories, all based on the same sources, should be so different poses some interesting problems in historiographic interpretation. One element in any such explanation will have to be the semantic problem. The word democracy simply means different things to different people. It meant one thing to the Greek philosophers who coined the word, and another to the Latins who borrowed it. It meant very similar things to educated men of the sixteenth century, who had been steeped in the writings of the ancient thinkers. Calvin, for example, almost certainly derived his understanding of the meaning of the word democracy and of the labels for various other forms of government from the writings of Aristotle and Cicero. Included in this volume are excerpts from key writings of both these ancient authorities to help the reader understand the meanings Calvin intended to convey in the passages upon which so many modern students of the problem base their theories.

These excerpts will make it clear that democracy, in the sixteenth century, referred to a form of government in which all the people shared the exercise of power. When this popular form of government proved to be beneficient, it was normally called a polity; when it degenerated into chaotic mob rule, it was often called a democracy. Moderns tend to give the word democracy the positive content which the ancients usually reserved for the word polity.

Even this clarification will not entirely resolve the semantic problem, however. In modern times the term democracy has developed many more layers of meaning. It has come to mean more than a form of government in which all the people share the rule. It also has come to imply the methods by which that form of government historically has been established, often by the method of popular revolution. Furthermore, it has come to mean certain mechanisms by which popular sharing in rule is realized, such as elections or representative bodies. Finally, it has come to suggest, particularly in Anglo-Saxon countries, the existence of certain basic individual rights or civil liberties which really limit the sovereign will of the majority and thereby prevent that majority from imposing its wishes in all circumstances. In other words, it implies the existence of safeguards which, in order to protect individual liberty, limit democracy itself. Recently certain radical groups have tried to revive the idea of direct democracy, challenging the principle of representation and arguing that all major decisions, at least, should be referred to the people for determination in what amounts to a continuing plebiscite. To the radical left this is the only true democracy.

This means that in trying to assess the influence of Calvin's ideas on later democracy, the modern scholar must go beyond Calvin's own specific uses of the term, and examine other passages in which he discusses political matters. Several of the commentators included in this volume have done this. In deciding what parts of Calvin's thought on politics can be used fairly to illuminate his opinion of democracy, these modern commentators have inevitably, and perhaps even unconsciously, been influenced by the meanings attached to democracy in their own societies. The determination and analysis of these influences can be a fascinating intellectual exercise.

A second method for studying the connection between Calvin and democracy is to consider the political implications of his religious views. He was, after all, primarily the leader of a religious movement. His writings were almost entirely devoted to religious topics. The really important influences he may have exercised on the politics of his followers may derive less from his random comments on politics, than from the great central doctrines and assumptions of his theological system. Influences of this sort would obviously be indirect. In fact, they might even have been unconscious, with Calvin never intending a given doctrine to have political significance, and his followers never realizing that they derived their political principles from his thoughts. But influences of this sort can, nevertheless, be powerful. In an age and among people dominated by religion, the basic presuppositions which people take for granted and of which they are barely aware, are likely to be religious. If these presuppositions can be shown to suggest certain kinds of political ideas, it may be fair to regard the presuppositions, rather than any explicit political teachings, as the fundamental source of the movement's political ideas.

There are several ways one might apply this method to Calvin. One would be to contemplate the political implications of his doctrine of predestination—that God elects a small group of people to become His "saints," and enjoy eternal bliss with Him in heaven, while He destines everyone else to eternal damnation. The view that this doctrine implies political rule by the saints, a kind of religious aristocracy, rather than democracy, is considered by several of our authors. Another possibility would be to examine the political implications of the basic Protestant doctrine of the "priesthood of all believers," the doctrine that every believer can have direct access to God, and need not depend on a properly ordained priest or professional clergyman as an intermediary, and that every believer can find the essential meaning of the Christian message for himself, by his own study of the Bible. The possibility that this implies individualism, and hence democracy, is explored by M. Charles Mercier, who wrote at a time when individual rights were being eroded everywhere by a rising tide of totalitarianism.

A third method for studying the connection between Calvin and democracy is to go beyond what he said to what he did. Actions sometimes speak louder than words, and Calvin was always more than a preacher and writer. He was also an ecclesiastical statesman, who, in order to advance his program for religious reformation, became involved in a great deal of political activity. That involvement was most intense in Geneva, where he personally built and directed a new Reformed Church, in constant collaboration with the city councils, and where he even occasionally served the city government in other ways, as a lawyer or diplomat. Calvin's political involvement also was significant in other countries, since he received appeals for advice from the growing numbers of his followers who were trying to influence their governments to adopt Calvinist programs of Reformation, and from rulers anxious for guidance in changing religious establishments. There is ample record of these political activities of Calvin's, in his wide-ranging correspondence, and in various types of governmental records. In this material one can find Calvin's opinions of some of the actual governments with which he dealt. These opinions suggest which forms of government he preferred in actual practice. Several of our authors have explored this line of inquiry.

A fourth method, which again concentrates on what Calvin did rather than on what he said, is to examine the churches he established. Calvin spent most of his time as an ecclesiastical statesman, not in secular politics, but in the foundation and guidance of churches. These churches had to be set up on organizational principles of some sort. The principles he recommended were frequently of a type which can be labeled representative or even democratic. Individual local churches were normally ruled by bodies called consistories or companies; churches in small areas were ruled by bodies called colloquies, or classes, or presbyteries; churches in large areas such as provinces or nations were ruled by bodies called synods or assemblies. The members of these bodies were usually chosen either by co-optation or by election or by some combination of these two methods. These bodies were thus established, to a certain degree at least, on representative and democratic principles of organization.

If it can be demonstrated that Calvinist ecclesiastical institutions were normally governed by democratic principles, this would suggest that they may have provided a model for secular democratic institutions. People who had grown accustomed to organizing their churches along democratic lines presumably might have found it logical and easy to reorganize their secular governments along the same lines. The possibility of drawing this kind of connection, based on analogies between ecclesiastical and political institutions, is explored in an article by Professor Robert M. Kingdon which has been excerpted in this volume.

* * *

The second obvious way of investigating the connections between Calvinism and democracy is to concentrate one's attention on the political ideas and actions of organized groups of Calvinists. This approach appeals to historians who believe that social forces have important influences on history. They point out that even the most charismatic leader does not stimulate precisely the same reactions in all of his followers in every time and place. They further argue that to appreciate the political implications of an ideology, one must study the political context in which it developed and had its roots. Finally, they contend that one must also study the political institutions which served as carriers for this ideology, since they could have influenced its impact in significant ways. These contexts and carriers must be studied in various times and places. The action of Calvinism within them should also be compared to the action of other ideologies in similar circumstances, in order to judge the degree to which Calvinism was unique.

Herbert Darling Foster's study of the political thought and practice of pre-American Calvinism, portions of which are included in this volume, is a grandiose and sweeping attempt at this sort of interpretation. However, in his attempt to demonstrate the direct relationship between Calvinism and democracy, Foster tends to ignore or at least minimize the differences in contexts and carriers which many later scholars feel existed between various national expressions of Calvinist Protestantism. Relating Calvinist theory to Calvinist action in several different countries, he points out the connection between Calvinist ideology on the one hand and constitutional resistance and representative government on the other. And, he argues, behind it all lay the dynamics of Calvinism: the trained conscience, mind, and will of clear-headed, fiercely self-disciplined men of affairs who possessed a sturdy sense of vocation and a well-defined concept of responsibility to God and the people.

Of course, to investigate completely and thoroughly the connection between Calvinism and democracy by using this approach, would require a vast program of empirical research, ranging over a period of two hundred years and over at least a dozen countries. A modest start toward such a research project can be made, however, by the judicious use of the case-study method. There are, in fact, already a significant number of case studies of this sort, linking Calvinism to political action in specific areas and at specific times. Several of them are included in this volume, and they represent three different applications of this basic approach.

A first application examines the political consequences of the development of Calvinism in certain cities. Calvin first adopted Protestant ideas and observed functioning Protestant churches in two Germanic free cities—in Basel, where he spent some time in study, and in Strasbourg, where he served as pastor of the French refugees' church. He developed his ideas further and had a chance to apply them in yet another free city—Geneva. He won much of his earliest and most enduring support in cities, both free ones like these and others subject to higher authorities. Some of the countries which were most responsive to his teachings were in the process of becoming more urban. Thus, in some ways Calvinism can be regarded as an urban ideology. The political components of this ideology therefore may reflect the political needs of certain kinds of early modern cities. In particular, they may reflect the needs of many of these cities to involve many of their citizens in the decision-making processes and to resist effectively the ever more threatening pressures of central governments of the monarchical type. In an article excerpted here, Dr. Hans Baron, an authority on the development and use of ideologies in cities of the Renaissance and Reformation period, suggests the possibilities of applying this approach to the study of Calvinist politics. By a close examination of certain key passages in the writings of the Strasbourg reformer, Martin Bucer, and of certain parallel passages in the writings of Calvin, he suggests ways in which urban political ideas entered Calvinist thought. He then goes on to point out ways in which they were adapted by Calvin to larger contexts, to governments controlling more power and territory than the governments of city states. It is certainly significant for the basic question raised in this volume, if it can be demonstrated that Calvin and his followers found these urban ideas acceptable and adaptable while other religious movements did not.

A second application concentrates on the political factions, generally led by aristocrats, which adopted Calvinism as one of several tools in their struggle for control of central governments. There were several such factions active in sixteenth-century Europe, most commonly at a time when a central government was weak. Among them were the Lords of the Congregation in Scotland, who led a revolt against the regency ruling for Mary, Queen of Scots, in 1558; the Huguenots in France, who went to war against the powers controlling the government of another minor king, Charles IX, in 1562; the Beggars in the Netherlands, who began agitation against the government of the absentee King Philip II in 1567, and resorted to war in 1572. In an article excerpted here, Professor H. G. Koenigsberger, an authority on the development of representative political institutions in the early modern period, examines the actions and ideologies of several of these factions. He discovers that both the Huguenots and the Beggars developed many of the characteristics of revolutionary democratic parties, anticipating in many interesting ways the Jacobin party which developed in France during the great revolution of the eighteenth century. But Koenigsberger also points out that the French Catholic League developed many of the same characteristics. Indeed, in its organization of the city of Paris during the late 1580's, the League anticipated the democratic Jacobins more closely than any Protestant faction of the period. This fact creates serious problems for those who would derive revolutionary democracy from something unique to Calvinism. It suggests that the democratic tendencies undeniably exhibited by groups of Calvinists at various times, were more the result of special political circumstances than of anything inherent in Calvinism.

A third application of this second approach concentrates on one particular event in which significant groups of Calvinists were involved and tries to establish both their responsibility for that event and the degree to which it may have been important in the development of modern democracy. Professor Michael Walzer, an authority on the history of radical political thought, adopts elements of this approach, in the study of which portions are included here. The event Walzer has chosen to study is the Puritan Revolution in seventeenth-century England. He believes this revolution to have been unique among religious upheavals of the period. He sees it as an essentially modern revolution, which sought to change existing society radically by creating for it new political institutions, and thereby became a model for later democratic revolutions. He traces a number of ways in which he believes Calvinist ideology was significantly adapted, revised, and refined by the English Puritans, who ended by turning it into an ideology far more revolutionary than the one developed by Calvin and his immediate followers a century before.

* * *

Altogether there have been suggested here seven ways in which the connections between Calvinism and democracy can be and have been explored, four attempting to link Calvin himself with democracy, three attempting to link organized Calvinism with democracy. Readers of this volume are provided with samples of every one of these seven. In some cases the sample is presented in pure form; in other cases several methods are combined in one sample. These materials make it possible for the reader to weigh for himself the persuasiveness of each of these ways of connecting the two phenomena, and the conclusions toward which each method points. He should be able to judge each method's inherent plausibility and its value when applied to this particular problem. This exercise should sharpen the reader's appreciation of the general problems involved in historians' attempts to resolve issues of this sort. Hopefully, however, his interest in this particular problem will also be whetted, so that he will move from considerations of method to considerations of substance. He should finally be able to make his own more informed judgment on the central theme of this volume: were Calvin and Calvinism sources of democracy?

CONFLICT OF OPINION

Extremes:

The fanatic for Calvinism was a fanatic for liberty; and, in the moral warfare for freedom, his creed was his most faithful counsellor and his never-failing support.

The Puritans, rallying upon those [industrious] classes, planted in their hearts the undying principles of democratic liberty.

—GEORGE BANCROFT

In its initial form Calvinism not only included a condemnation of resistance but it lacked all leaning toward liberalism, constitutionalism, or representative principles. Where it had free range it developed characteristically into a theocracy, a kind of oligarchy maintained by an alliance of the clergy and gentry from which the mass of the people was excluded and which was, in general, illiberal, oppressive, and reactionary.

—GEORGE H. SABINE

Did Calvin himself favor democracy as a form of government?

Calvin was as much in favor of the democratic form as he was opposed to the monarchical one.

Calvin was a great propagator of democracy, but he energetically tried to ward off its abuses and excesses.

—ÉMILE DOUMERGUE

From considering only his political ideas, one would certainly be entitled to conclude that Calvin was not a precursor of modern democracy.

—CHARLES MERCIER

If Calvin mixes democratic elements with aristocratic constitutions, he nevertheless remains completely foreign to the dogmas of modern democracy . . . he does not believe either in popular sovereignty or in individual rights.

—MARC-EDOUARD CHENEVIÈRE

As an ideal form, Calvin wavers between pure aristocracy and a mixed form of aristocracy and democracy. Despite this obvious fact, there persist among Calvin scholars assertions which depict Calvin as favoring either a pure democracy or a pure aristocracy and correspondingly speak of a democratic or aristocratic principle in him.

—JOSEF BOHATEC

"Democracy" is not a term in favor with Calvin. He does not advocate democracy in and of itself: he fears its deterioration into anarchy. Nevertheless, his notion of "aristocracy tempered by democracy" approaches our conception of representative democracy. It becomes unmistakably clear in his later writings that the ideal basis of government is election by the citizens.

—JOHN T. MCNEILL

Beyond the shadow of a doubt, the elders really represent the Church, which delegates to them its sovereignty. The theory of the representative system is really a Calvinist theory.

—EMILE DOUMERGUE

One believes oneself dreaming, when one learns from M. Doumergue, that "authentic Calvinist conceptions" are "at the origin of the representative system." Even if one gives to the role of the community in the Calvinist Church its largest sense, and even if one neglects the important restrictions on it stipulated by Calvin, one still searches in vain for any new principles this conception would bring to republican Geneva.

—GEORGES DE LAGARDE

Was Calvinist thought the principal inspiration for the earliest 'democratic' revolts against authoritarian governments in Europe?

Calvinist political thought helped more than any other tendency of the time to prevent a full victory of absolutism, and to prepare the way for constitutional and even republican ideas.

—HANS BARON

Religion was the binding force that held together the divergent interests of the different classes and provided them with an organization and a propaganda machine capable of creating the first genuinely national and international parties in modern European history, . . . and popular democratic tyranny appeared both in Calvinist Ghent and Catholic Paris.

—H. G. KOENIGSBERGER

It will be argued below that it was the Calvinists who first switched the emphasis of political thought from the prince to the saint (or band of saints) and then constructed a theoretical justification for independent political action.

—MICHAEL WALZER

A modern moral:

If in our time the realm of politics is to be redeemed from corruption and triviality and snarling partisanship, the church has a function to perform that it has too much neglected. It will not be a waste of time to sit for a while at Calvin's feet.

—JOHN T. MCNEILL

A TABLE OF MEN, BOOKS, AND TERMS

ALTHUSIUS, JOHANNES (1557–1638): German Calvinist lawyer and public official who wrote extensively to defend the political course of the Dutch Calvinists in their struggle with Spain.

AMBOISE, CONSPIRACY OF, MAY, 1560: an abortive attempt by a small group of hotheaded young Calvinist noblemen to kidnap the French king (Francis II) and place France under the guidance of his Protestant cousin, the Prince de Condé.

BEZA, THEODORE (1519–1605): French-born Calvinist clergyman and, after 1564, Calvin's successor as leader of the Geneva Company of Pastors.

BOURBON: family name of those descendants of Hugh Capet who ruled France from the accession of Henry IV in 1589, until the establishment of the First Republic in 1792, and again from 1814–1848.

BUCER, MARTIN (also Butzer and Kulhorn) (1491–1551): close friend of Calvin and the leading Protestant Reformer of Strasbourg from 1527 to 1548.

BUCHANAN, GEORGE (c. 1506–1582): Scottish humanist and tutor of James VI of Scotland (later James I of England) who allegedly was influenced by Calvinism to advocate popular sovereignty.

BULLINGER, HENRY (1504–1575): after 1531, Zwingli's successor as leader of the Reformation in Zürich.

CALVIN, JOHN (1509–1564): leader of the Reformation in Geneva from 1541 until 1564, and founder of the Presbyterian and Reformed churches.

CATHOLIC LEAGUE: founded in 1576 as a party of the nobility with the essentially conservative aim of preserving the privileges of the Roman Catholic Church in France.

CHANDIEU, ANTOINE DE LA ROCHE (c. 1534–1591): French Reformed pastor of noble birth who staunchly defended the presbyterian church polity of Calvin and Beza in his native land.

CHARLES I (reigned 1625–1649): son of James I and second Stuart king of England; executed for treason by the victorious Parliamentarians at the conclusion of the Civil War in 1649.

CHARLES V (reigned 1519–1556): head of the House of Hapsburg and Holy Roman Emperor.

CHARLES IX (reigned 1560–1574): king of France; second son of Henry II and Catherine de Medici.

COLIGNY, GASPARD DE (1519–1572): Count of Châtillon and Admiral of France, a nephew of the powerful Constable Anne de Montmorency, and one of the key leaders of the Huguenots who was murdered during the St. Bartholomew's Day Massacre, August 24, 1572.

COLLOQUY: in the French Reformed churches, an ecclesiastical body made up of all the ministers and chosen lay representatives from each parish in a given area, corresponding to the presbytery in Scottish and American Presbyterianism.

COMPANY OF PASTORS: in the Genevan Church, all of the ordained ministers of the city-state who held weekly meetings to care for matters related to preaching the Gospel, administering the sacraments, and guiding the moral life of the faithful.

CONDÉ: title of one branch of the Bourbon family, princes of the blood, which provided leadership for the Huguenot cause in France during the latter half of the sixteenth century after the conversion of the first Prince de Condé (Louis I de Bourbon, d. 1569) to the Calvinist faith.

CONGREGATIONAL: that form of church polity based on the premise that each individual congregation is self-governing according to democratic principles and procedures, roughly corresponding to democracy in the political realm.

CONSISTORY: in the Genevan and French Reformed churches, a local ecclesiastical body made up of the resident pastor or pastors and representative laymen who met regularly to care for the discipline of the congregation.

COUNCIL OF SIXTY: in Geneva in the sixteenth-century, an elected advisory council of relatively little importance which stood between the much more powerful Little Council and Council of Two Hundred.

COUNCIL OF TWO HUNDRED: instituted in Geneva in 1527 and elected by the General Assembly of all the citizens, it became a policy making body for the Genevan state in the sixteenth-century.

CROMWELL, OLIVER (1599–1658): longtime Member of Parliament, general in the Parliamentary Army during the English Civil War, Lord Protector of the English Commonwealth from 1653 to 1658, and staunch Calvinist layman.

DUPLESSIS-MORNAY, PHILIPPE, see Philippe du Plessis Mornay.

ELDERS: in the Reformed and Presbyterian churches the lay leaders of the local congregations, who in the sixteenth century were sometimes chosen directly by the entire membership and sometimes indirectly by a self-perpetuating church council (consistory or session) made up of the minister and lay representatives.

ENGLISH REVOLUTION OF 1640 (also the Great Rebellion or the English Civil War): beginning with the Long Parliament of 1640, with actual hostilities breaking out in 1642, and concluding in 1649 with the victory of the Puritan-backed Parliamentarians over the Royalists.

EPISCOPAL: that form of church polity based on the premise that the church should be governed by bishops, roughly corresponding to monarchy in the political realm.

FAREL, WILLIAM (1489–1565): French-born Protestant Reformer who aided Calvin in establishing the Reformation in Geneva in the years 1536 to 1538.

FRANCIS I (reigned 1515–1547): Valois king of France, Renaissance monarch and the ruler to whom Calvin dedicated his *Institutes*.

FRANCIS II (reigned 1559–1560): Valois king of France who acceded to the throne at the age of fifteen and who was dominated throughout his reign by the Guise family.

GENERAL ASSEMBLY OF THE CITIZENS OF GENEVA: the assembly of all the citizens summoned only when grave decisions affecting all had to be made; supposedly the repository of ultimate political sovereignty in the Genevan state.

GOODMAN, CHRISTOPHER (1520–1603): English Calvinist and Marian exile who wrote a politically incendiary book entitled *How Superior Powers ought to be obeyed* in 1558 in which he argued that under certain conditions Christians could engage in popular revolution.

GUISE: a noble French family, closely related to the dukes of Lorraine, which was able to wield tremendous power and influence in sixteenth-century France through marriage into the royal family, extensive service to the French monarchs, and the careful acquisition of local patronage; leaders of the Catholic League during the Wars of Religion and sworn enemies of the Huguenots.

HENRY II (reigned 1547–1559): Valois king of France, son of Francis I, father of Francis II, Charles IX and Henry III, and vigorous opponent of French Calvinism.

HENRY III (reigned 1574–1589): last Valois king of France and third son of Henry II to mount the French throne. He was assassinated by a demented Dominican friar in August, 1589.

HENRY IV (formerly Henry of Navarre) (reigned 1589–1610): first Bourbon king of France who in 1593 renounced his Calvinist faith in order to secure the acceptance of his rule by rank-and-file Frenchmen; assassinated in 1610 by a Catholic fanatic.

HENRY VIII (reigned 1509–1547): second Tudor king of England under whom the Protestant Reformation was introduced.

HENRY OF NAVARRE: see Henry IV.

HOTMAN, FRANCIS (1524–1590): French Calvinist scholar, publicist and jurist who in 1573 published *Franco-Gallia* in which he espoused the principles of constitutional monarchy.

HUGUENOT: a word of unknown origin (perhaps from the German word *Eidgenossen,* meaning "confederates") which in sixteenth-century France came to designate the French Protestants, both religiously and politically.

INSTITUTES OF THE CHRISTIAN RELIGION: Calvin's most famous work which he first published in 1536 and which went through many editions before its final revision in 1560; perhaps the most influential book of the Reformation era.

JAMES I (also James VI of Scotland, 1567–1625) (reigned 1603–1625): cousin of Elizabeth Tudor and first Stuart king of England.

KNOX, JOHN (c. 1514–1572): Scottish Calvinist minister and key figure in establishing the Reformed Kirk in Scotland.

LAUD, WILLIAM (1573–1645): Charles I's advisor on all matters of religion, relentless foe of Puritans and other Dissenters, and Archbishop of Canterbury from 1633 to 1645 when he was charged with treason and ordered beheaded by the English Parliament.

L'ESTOILE, PIERRE DE (1546–1611): professor of law and foremost teacher of jurisprudence in France in his day who, although a devout conservative, bitterly opposed the Catholic League and the Guise.

LITTLE COUNCIL: in Geneva in the sixteenth-century, the council composed of four syndics, their four latest predecessors, the city treasurer (all elected popularly), and sixteen others chosen by the Council of Two Hundred which carried on the day-to-day business of the state.

LUTHER, MARTIN (1483–1546): German Reformer who touched off the Protestant Reformation by posting his Ninety-Five Theses at Wittenberg in 1517.

MAGISTRATE: common sixteenth-century term for any civil official who was empowered to administer and enforce the law of the land.

MAYENNE, DUC DE (1554–1611): Charles de Guise, member of the powerful Guise family who became the leader of the Catholic League after his older brother's assassination by an agent of Henry III of France in 1588.

MEDICI, CATHERINE DE (1519–1598): descendant of the famous Florentine Medicis and wife of Henry II of France who was very active and influential in French politics during the reigns of her three sons: Francis II, Charles IX and Henry III.

MILTON, JOHN (1608–1674): English poet and philosopher who held many Calvinist views and who in many ways was the epitome of the religious ferment which accompanied the English Civil War.

MONTMORENCY, ANNE DE (1493–1567): Constable of France and head of one of the country's most powerful noble families.

MORÉLY, JEAN (also Morelli): sire de Villiers, a French nobleman who became a Calvinist about 1547, and subsequently one of the most articulate leaders of the congregational faction in the French Reformed Church from 1562 until his disappearance from the scene in 1572.

MORNAY, PHILIPPE DU PLESSIS: (also Philippe de Mornay) (1549–1623): Huguenot statesman, soldier and lay theologian who advocated representative government and constitutional limitation of monarchy.

PHILIP II (reigned 1556–1598): Hapsburg, son of Holy Roman Emperor Charles V, king of Spain and champion of the Roman Catholic faith in Europe in the last half of the sixteenth century.

POLITIQUES: the term used to describe those French Catholics who, after the St. Bartholomew's Day Massacre of 1572, felt that considerations of state and political unity were more important than any religious issues.

PONET, JOHN (c. 1514–1556): Edwardian bishop with Calvinist leanings who, while a Marian exile in Strasbourg, wrote the first book by an English Reformer condoning tyrannicide.

PRESBYTERIAN: that form of church polity based on the premise that the church should be governed by elders and ministers of equal rank, roughly corresponding to republicanism in the political realm.

PURITANS: those individuals within the Church of England in the sixteenth and seventeenth centuries who wanted to make the Church more Protestant and "purify" it of all Roman practices.

RAMUS, PETER (1515–1572): victim of the St. Bartholomew's Day Massacre in 1572 who had gained notoriety as an anti-Aristotelian philosophy professor at the University of Paris and as a lay leader of the congregationalist faction in the French Reformed Church.

REFORMED CHURCH: common self-designation of the Calvinist ecclesiastical bodies in countries like France, Germany, the Netherlands and Switzerland in the sixteenth century.

ROMANS 13: key passage in the New Testament in which Paul explains the obligation of the Christian to obey those in political power.

ROUSSEAU, JEAN-JACQUES (1712–1778): lineal descendant of French Huguenots and Genevan-born philosopher whose political writings supposedly influenced the men of the French Revolution of 1789.

SAINT BARTHOLOMEW'S DAY MASSACRE, August 24, 1572: when perhaps as many as 70,000 Huguenots were killed in France in an attempt to put an end to their religious and political influence in that country.

SAINTS: common Puritan term designating God's "Elect."

SYNDICS: in Geneva, the magistrates elected by the General Assembly of the citizens.

SYNOD: in the French Reformed Church, representative assemblies of the local congregations held at both the provincial and national level which met periodically to deal with ecclesiastical matters of provincial and national concern.

TROELTSCH, ERNST (1865–1923): German theologian and sociologist who in a number of essays argued that the Reformation produced an essentially authoritarian governmental structure, both in church and state.

VALOIS: family name of the French kings from Philip VI (1328–1350) to Henry III (1574–1589).

VENERABLE COMPANY OF PASTORS: see Company of Pastors.

VINDICIAE CONTRA TYRANNOS: famous Huguenot tract of undetermined authorship first published in 1579 which posited a contractual theory of government and argued for the right of inferior magistrates to lead popular revolutions against tyrannical monarchs.

WARS OF RELIGION IN FRANCE: a series of civil wars in France from 1562–1598 which had both religious and political ramifications.

WILLIAM OF ORANGE (also William of Nassau and the Prince of Orange) (1533–1584): leader of the Dutch Calvinists in their struggle for independence from Spain who in 1584 was assassinated by an agent of Philip II.

WILLIAMS, ROGER (1603–1684): English-born dissenting clergyman, founder of Rhode Island and staunch advocate of religious freedom who is sometimes placed in the Calvinist tradition.

ZWINGLI, ULRICH (1484–1531): the Protestant Reformer of Zürich whose followers gradually amalgamated with the Calvinists after his death on the battlefield in 1531.

CALVIN AND CALVINISM

Sources of Democracy?

1. GENERAL OPINIONS ON THE PROBLEM

Émile Doumergue

CALVIN A SOURCE OF DEMOCRACY

Émile Doumergue (1844–1937) was the greatest scholar on Calvin of his generation. He was born at Nîmes, the son of a Protestant pastor. After taking his theological training, Doumergue was himself ordained a minister of the French Reformed Church. In 1880, he became a professor on the Protestant Theological Faculty at Montauban. He earned the Dr. Theol. degree at the University of Geneva in 1901, and in 1907, was appointed dean of the Montauban Protestant Theological Faculty. He spent the remainder of his life at that French city, retiring in 1919, but continuing to teach part-time and to write until his death in 1937. His prolific scholarly career was climaxed by the publication of his monumental biography of Calvin in seven volumes from 1899–1927 entitled: *Jean Calvin, les hommes et les choses de son temps.* Although Doumergue has been often censured by modern scholars for his uncritical attitude toward his subject, his work on the Reformer of Geneva remains as the most painstaking, detailed, and precise biography of Calvin yet written.

BUT if the sovereign is not a monarch, what must he be? A magistrate elected by the people. Calvin was as much in favor of the democratic form as he was opposed to the monarchical one. . . .

Leaving aside the utopian Morelli and the fanatic anti-calvinist O. Douen, we will perhaps find it more surprising to see authors who merit respect for the calm of their learning, also speak in turn of the *anti-democratic* character of the work and thought of Calvin. M. de Crue: "*There is nothing democratic* in the Picard reformer." M. Lang: "Calvinism, but not Calvin, has a predisposition toward democracy." Troeltsch: "The personal conception of Calvin was as anti-democratic and authoritarian as possible." How can we explain this mystery?

First of all, and most importantly, because these authors, like the others, have not made a sufficiently complete study of Calvin's true thought. They are not aware of all the texts that we have just cited. They refer only to certain isolated excerpts and fail to achieve the total impression which alone is the true one.

In addition, some of the authors, and in particular Troeltsch, have allowed themselves to be misled by Rieker and the fundamental error that he has committed. With his great and justly deserved authority Rieker has spread an entirely false idea (we believe we have shown this) of the Church according to Calvin. Rieker only considered one half of the Calvinist conception and excluded the other which is no less important and no more open to question.

From Émile Doumergue, *Jean Calvin, les hommes et les choses de son temps,* V (Lausanne: Georges Bridel and Company, 1917), pp. 440, 450–453, 611–614, 701–706. Reprinted by permission of French Reproduction Rights, Inc. Translation by Malcolm Sylvers and Robert D. Linder. Documenting footnotes are preserved in this selection in special cases in order to clarify otherwise unidentified quotations. In all other selections, the footnotes have been omitted.

He has forgotten that the Church is not only a divine institution (from which one could deduce the aristocratic character of the Church), but also, equally and at the same time, an association of believers (from which fact the democratic and representative character of the Church necessarily follows). Since Calvin thus made the offices of the Church an institution of God, Troeltsch deduced that these offices were not linked to nomination by the community. He concluded that: "In this way the ecclesiastical constitution at Geneva was very aristocratic." This is completely inaccurate.

It is also necessary to note the influence of Galiffe's calumny, reproduced and transmitted by Kampschulte, on almost all authors, of what seems to be the true motto of autocracy: "It is always necessary to keep the people in poverty so that they remain obedient." But this is calumny and nothing more. Calvin did not wish either poverty or ignorance for the people. On the contrary, he never ceased to proclaim and to practice the great democratic principle of mass education. Thus, speaking of the prophets' schools, he declares that one must not spare any expense to pay those who have the gift of teaching. No doubt he had in mind primarily the pastors, but education must be extended to all. "Schools have been neglected and a crass ignorance has covered Christendom." If God wished to institute prophets' schools, he intended "that these prophets make the people participants in this knowledge." Everyone cannot be a prophet, "but *everyone* is a disciple of God." "It is necessary that *everyone* be educated by God," "not every one a doctor, but still not ignorant and stupid like beasts."

It is also necessary to recall up to what point Calvin proclaimed the inanity of human distinctions, titles, ranks, and human honors. "All shepherds and field laborers, all artisans and others like them must consider their condition to be holy." And again: "Neither God nor His gifts depend on humans. Experience shows that God does not give His gifts only, or always, to the rich, but on the contrary He gives them often to men who are not noble but have a lowly rank. He even calls men from the stables to supreme honors." All this is well known.

In addition when there was a discussion at Frankfort about a pastor, Calvin had recourse to a true referendum, to a plebiscite, and he made all the people vote in order to know if they wished or not to keep their pastor. He asked the people "spontaneously and freely" to give their opinion. He noted that the "majority of the suffrages" was for keeping the pastor, and that it pleased the "majority." Elsewhere he specifies that it is not necessary to demand that everyone approve the votes and the elections. But it is necessary to demand that everyone submit to the majority and that is what he did: "I accept the fact that not every individual has such good advice and discretion as to make the proper choice. For this reason it seems to me that one should be well satisfied if I accept the decision of the greatest number."

Is it necessary to recall the constant and pointed lessons in real democracy that Calvin's discipline gave every day? These were lessons not in egalitarianism but in the principle of equality before the law.

It is certainly tedious to have to repeat all of this. It ought to be for us to keep to Troeltsch's own declarations. He declares and repeats that "It is oligarchic rather than democratic," yet he recognizes that "despite (!) all, the ecclesiastical community in the republican city of Geneva strongly pushed, in the final analysis, toward democratic ideas and the principle of the sovereignty of the people." He recognizes that this influence was even further increased by the fact that the final and decisive means of exerting a pressure on political authority was "the appeal to the opinion of the people and the electors through the sermon." "'Appeal to the people' is in all difficult cases the *ultima ratio* of Calvin and his successors." He also recognizes that "the Calvinist Church is incontestably a Church community," and that from this flows "a democratic and constitutional character." Thus, in order to show the degree to which Calvin preferred democratic government both for the Church and the State, and to demonstrate the extent to which he has been the propagator of democratic ideas, it almost suffices for us simply to take advantage of the concessions that our opponents themselves have made.

After having repeated: "It [democracy] is against Calvinism's own will" (a more or less gratuitous hypothesis that the system-makers pass on from one to the other and which cannot be accepted), Troeltsch concludes: "It would thus be an error to find French or American modern democracy present purely and simply in Calvinism." Obviously! Calvin did not purely and simply create the present democracy in either France or America. This is not the question. But Troeltsch adds: "Calvinism has become the form of Christianity which today is intimately linked to the process of modern democratization. It can be in agreement with democracy without sacrificing the religious idea. At the same time, by its religious and even physical legitimization of the individual, by its maintenance of the essential inequality (?) of men, by its conservative sense of order and law, it has avoided the most dangerous consequences of democracy: government by mere number and abstract equality."

This conclusion is acceptable to us in so far as, having put aside what is vague and equivocal, it means that Calvin was a great supporter of democracy, while energetically trying to ward off the abuses and excesses. For us, the latter does not contradict the former, but rather reinforces it.

. . . Arriving after a time at the end of our study on "The Thought of Calvin," it is necessary for us to point out the influence of this thought on the present-day modern world. This should be a very revealing and worthwhile investigation. We will content ourselves with discussing three items: political influence, social influence, economic influence.

For political influence, limiting everything to the subject at hand, we will point out only the relation between the Calvinism of Calvin and the Declaration of the Rights of Man of 1789. The Declaration of the Rights of Man of 1789 is the result of the bringing together at Paris of two streams. And the first of these streams is the Calvinist stream, with three easily discernible currents.

The first current flows directly from Calvin through Theodore Beza, Hotman, Duplessis-Mornay, to Jurieu and so forth.

The second current flows from Calvin through Knox and Goodman, into Scotland, then into England, to the Puritans, who manifested, that is to say, proclaimed "not only the spirit, but likewise the letter of the revolutionary theories of the eighteenth-century"[1] (including native-rights, birth-rights and universal suffrage).

The Puritan effort half succeeded and half failed. The current was split into two: it resulted in the English current and the American current.

In England the theories of the Scottish Calvinists led to the "Glorious Revolution" of 1688, which is in essence, as acknowledged by M. Boutmy, a triumph of Calvinist ideas (the contract theory of government, the declaration of rights). This was the constitutionalism of the Presbyterians, with Locke serving as theoretician. In Locke, son of Puritan parents, blended the tendencies of the Puritans and the latitudinarianism of the Church of England.

And the ideas of Locke crossed over to France, or to say it more plainly, they overran France in the eighteenth century. A cloud of works introduced the French to English political concepts, and even more important, there were all the trips to England by the leaders of eighteenth-century political philosophy to initiate themselves first hand into the ideas which they diffused afterwards with such an impact. Jules Barni, an admirer of the eighteenth century, writes: "The philosophical movement of the eighteenth century is essentially a French movement," but he adds: "It is from England that the French writers Montesquieu, Voltaire, Rousseau re-

[1] From Charles Borgeaud, *Annales de l'école libre des sciences politiques*, 1892, p. 145.

ceived their first impulse, or drew their principle models."

Montesquieu lived in England for two years, 1729–1731, and became completely enamored with the English system of government. Voltaire spent three years in England. "That was, as he put it, his hegira." "It is to the English sage Locke, as he himself called him, that it is necessary to go back to, in part at least, for the source of the powerful influence exercised by Voltaire upon the formation of the modern spirit. But this point is well established and I do not have to dwell upon it."[2] And finally Rousseau, the Genevan, borrowed extensively from Locke for his *Émile*. And Jules Barni concludes: "Perhaps Locke justly can be considered the father of eighteenth-century philosophy. . . . And as it is the Reformation, as it is the triumph of the Protestant spirit which made England what it was then, it follows that in this manner the philosophical movement of the eighteenth century is connected with the religious movement of the sixteenth century."—"connected with . . .;" we say no more and no less and here we do not inquire into what was the exact nature of this tie.

But the triumph of the "constitutionalism" of the Presbyterians coincided with the defeat of the "democracy" of the Independents. The latter fled to America aboard the *Mayflower*. And it is the third current of which we have spoken, the American current. The "Fundamental Orders" of Connecticut, adopted on January 14, 1639, has been called "the first written constitution of modern democracy." It was of the spirit of Beza, of Duplessis-Mornay, of Jurieu. Roger Williams, the preacher of Harlem,[3] founded Providence and, in 1647, its constitution was ratified fixing "the first great date in the history of modern democracy."[4]

And then this Calvinist-American current crossed anew the ocean, coming to inundate France with even greater consequences than was the case of the Calvinist-English current. It is a historian, also a little inclined to minimize the originality of the French Revolution and to stress the importance of religious and Calvinist ideas, M. Aulard who says: "America contributed to a republicanizing of French sentiments in a much more immediate and effective way [than England] by a lively example." Franklin says: "The French read with enthusiasm the constitutions of our newly independent colonies." Mirabeau himself writes in a mood of uncertainty: "One properly applauds in a general way the lofty manifesto of the United States of America," and is frightened by it. Condorcet writes: "The act which declared the independence of America is a simple and sublime exposition of those rights so sacred and so long forgotten. In no other nation have they been so fully realized, nor conserved with such perfect integrity."

French translations of the "Bill of Rights" follow. Systematic propaganda is organized, with a secret committee, a clandestine communications network. Lafayette leaves for America. It is "the American inoculation," in the words of Mallet du Pan; it is "the American era," according to Lafayette. It is he who will present for the first time a Declaration plan to the constituent assembly, and he will acknowledge later that his model was the Declaration of Virginia. Constituent deputy Lameth declares—it is the opinion of his contemporaries—that "the Constitution of the United States supplied the idea." A journalist of 1789 was of the opinion "that if in the new hemisphere the brave inhabitants of Philadelphia have given an example of a people who recovered their liberty, France ought to convey it to the remainder of the world." And the reporter of the committee on the constitution, the Archbishop of Bordeaux, expressed himself thusly on July 27, 1789: "This idea [of making a Declaration of Rights], conceived in another hemisphere, ought to be transplanted here in our land. . . . America has shown us upon which principles we ought to rest the preservation of our liberty; and it is the new world, where in times past we had shown no

[2] From Henri Marion, *J. Locke*, 1893 pp. 81–82.
[3] Here Doumergue meant "the preacher of Salem."
[4] From Borgeaud, *op. cit.*

zeal for chains, which teaches us today so that we will not bring misfortune upon ourselves." Thus it was an archbishop who made this allusion to the enslaving influence of Catholic Spain and to the liberating influence of Protestant and Calvinist America.

. . . It remains to be said what this spirit has done in the world, not only according to some theologians or some sociologists, or according to some makers of systems called metaphysics, but also according to the historians, recounting the facts, the events in the life of peoples and of mankind. This will be the concern of another work. By way of conclusion, we must limit ourselves to indicating the judgments of some of these historians, chosen from among those whose authority is unquestionable and unquestioned.

1. In the first place, we would make the point that we are talking about a moment that is unique in history. "It was a moment when all of Europe was awakened from its political and social slumber, as much as from its religious and intellectual sleep. And this Frenchman, Calvin, seized the unique occasion, upon the authority of God, to lead the march, to guide toward the objective."[5]

2. He leads. An American, Professor Glasgow, has said: "It is only through Calvinism that the 'Psalm of liberty' found its way from troubled consciences to the lips, and Calvinism, in fact, has triumphed and guaranteed constitutional liberty for mankind." A German, Erhardt: "He knew how to appreciate the importance of all kinds of human labor, he knew how to appreciate the historical legitimacy of new social conditions and the independence of his views is such that, in fact, his economic ideas contain nothing of the ideas of the Middle Ages. . . . We are not able to acknowledge it fully. Calvin, by the rationality of his views, by his independence from the traditional prejudices, by his profound knowledge of social life, of its nature, of its relationships of the exigencies of production and consumption, was for the most part well ahead of his contemporaries." A Belgian, Professor Friedericq, has said: "Calvin appears at precisely the moment when self-government seems about to expire in the West, hardly more than barely preserved in a few poor and obscure Swiss cantons. Calvin frees the Church from temporal power and establishes a religious organization free of the entire Roman hierarchy. Each Calvinist parish is a little egalitarian and autonomous republic, ruled by universal suffrage. . . . It is an unexpected return to self-government, vanquished and almost extirpated in the political realm, but returning again in the religious domain. At the end of the sixteenth century, all of Catholic, Lutheran and Anglican Europe once more is surrendered to monarchy which is more or less absolute. But at the same time there are already three centers of self-government issuing from Calvinism: Switzerland, Holland and Scotland. And these three little centers of political liberty, which occupy such a small portion of the map of Europe, soon radiate over all of the West and over the entire world. . . . Indeed, the philosophers and the encyclopedists were hardly Calvinists. But from whence have the great French thinkers derived their doctrines, so new and bold for France, so contrary to those of the preceding generation in their own country, so radically opposed to the principles of the 'Splendid Century' of Louis XIV? They are derived, undeniably, from Calvinist sources."

Finally an Englishman, John Richard Green (1837–1883), the author of an extensive history of the English people, after having called the ecclesiastical organization of Calvin "a Christian republic," adds: "It is into Calvinism that the modern world plunges its roots. For it is Calvinism which first reveals the dignity and worth of man. Called of God, heir of heaven, the merchant in his shop and the peasant in his field suddenly become the equal of noble and king."

3. Thus Calvin leads, and Holland follows. "The Reformation entered the Low Countries by way of the Walloon

[5] From G. Boardmann Eager, "Calvin as a Civic and Social Influence," *The Review and Expositer*, 1909, p. 557.

door" (that is to say, Calvinism).[6] And the great historian of Holland, Motley, says: "More than any other group, Calvinism is responsible for the political liberties of Holland, England and America." Groen van Prinsterer: "In Calvinism lies the origin and the guarantee of our constitutional liberties." And M. Kuyper, the former prime minister of Holland: "Historically, Calvinism dug the canal into which flowed the Reformation inasmuch as it was neither Lutheran, nor Anabaptist, nor Socinian. And politically, it shapes this movement which has guaranteed the liberty of nations under a constitutional regime."

4. Calvin leads, and England follows. Sir James Stephen, the celebrated statesman, churchman, jurist and professor of modern history at Cambridge, speaking of the organization set up by the national synod in France in 1559, says: "Thus a great revolution had been accomplished. At the center of the French monarchy, Calvin and his disciples had established a spiritual republic and solemnly acknowledged four foundational principles, each of which would have far reaching consequences of the greatest importance for political society." (He is concerned with the role of the will of the people, the delegation of powers by the people, the equality of clergy and laity, and the mutual independence of church and state.)

Comparing Hobbes, Cromwell and Calvin, John Morley, statesman and publicist, says: "Hobbes and Cromwell were giants, each in his own way. But if we consider their powers of recruiting and organizing men in an enduring fashion, their influence upon the convictions, morals and conduct of great masses of men, generation after generation, . . . the imprint which they have left upon social and political institutions in those places where the Protestant faith prevails, from the country of John Knox to the country of Jonathan Edwards, it is necessary to note well, compared to Calvin, not concerning their intellectual capacities, but concerning their power to shape a world, Hobbes and Cromwell are hardly any more than names written on the surface of the water."

With William III of Orange, Dutch Calvinism and English Calvinism effect their junction. "It was the battle of the Boyne in Ireland in 1690, which in truth decided the kind of Protestantism which would prevail, not only in Great Britain, but in America and in the world. For if William had been defeated, Protestantism would not have found a shelter upon the face of the earth."[7] Now at the Boyne, there were two heads.—William! "The dogma of predestination formed the keystone of his religion. Often he was heard to declare that if he had to abandon that doctrine, he would lose his faith in an all-powerful Providence and become a simple Epicurean."[8]—Schomberg! "A Dutchman and a Frenchman, that being said for the immortal glory of both countries."[9] With them were all Protestantism. "There was hardly a Protestant Church, or a Protestant nation, which was not represented in this army which a strange succession of events had brought together on the most remote island of the West to fight for the Protestant religion."[10] Half was English, the other half was Scottish, Dutch, German, Danish, Finnish plus, above all, Huguenots from France and Irishmen from Ulster. And the motto was "Westminister," "the word that has been the symbol of the English Calvinist churches, before and since."[11] . . .

5. Calvin leads, and eighteenth-century Europe follows England and Calvin. "The study of English institutions by Montesquieu, Turgot, Voltaire and Rousseau gave form and direction to the French Revolution."[12]

6. Finally, Calvin leads, and America follows. Rufus Choate (1799–1869),

[6] From Frank T. Glasgow, "Calvin's Influence Upon the Political Development of the World," in *Calvin Memorial Addresses at Savannah,* 1909, p. 187.

[7] From T. B. Macaulay, *Histoire d'Angleterre,* trans. by de Peyronnet, 1861, II, 365.
[8] From Glasgow, *op. cit.,* p. 186.
[9] From *Ibid.,* p. 185.
[10] From T. B. Macaulay, *Histoire d'Angleterre,* trans. by A. Pichot, 1861, V, 117.
[11] From Glasgow, *op. cit.,* p. 185.
[12] From A. V. Hiester, "Calvin and Civil Liberty," *The Reformed Church Review,* 1909, p. 312.

the great American jurist, returning to the years 1553–1558, to the flight of the English from their own country and to their refuge in Geneva, says: "I attribute to those five years at Geneva, an influence which changed the face of the world. I believe I am able to trace back to them the great English Civil War, the republican constitution, elaborated upon in the cabin of the *Mayflower*, the theology of Jonathan Edwards, the battle of Bunker Hill and the independence of America." Bancroft, the great American historian, political figure and ambassador, says: "We republicans ought not to forget that Calvin was not only the founder of a sect; above all, he was among the legislators of modern republicanism . . . he was from the impregnable fortress of Geneva, the focal point of democracy. . . . The fanatic for Calvinism was a fanatic for liberty; and, in the moral warfare for freedom, his creed was his most faithful counsellor and his never-failing support." Dr. Smith, author of an extremely remarkable work entitled *The Creeds of Presbyterians*, says: "The fathers of our republic . . . had a model. In the shaping of our republic, the framers of the Constitution of the United States borrowed heavily from the constitution of the Presbyterian churches of Scotland." "John Calvin," says Ranke, "was virtually the founder of America."

7. Calvin is leading, and continues to lead. More and more he is leading the churches. One after another, the Lutheran churches are adopting the presbyterian synodal organization and switching to the diaconate of Calvin. In their turn, the Anglican churches, and even the Catholic churches (in their own way), are seeing the only salvation of the Christian Church in the modern world in this social and charitable organization of lay forces.

And if Calvin is still one of the most ignored and detested of men, it would not be so if he were more carefully studied. In those places where his person and works are not slandered, they are beginning to find respect and esteem, and for all that, the influence of his thought is growing and will continue to grow. One might say that the hour of justice and retribution is at hand.

Georges de Lagarde

CALVIN NO SOURCE OF DEMOCRACY

Georges de Lagarde (1898–1967) was born in Chambéry in Savoy, the son of a professional soldier. He spent most of his life in Paris where he pursued legal studies at the *Institut Catholique* and earned his doctorate in law from the University of Paris. After serving in the French army in World War I, he became chief of the legal department of the Mines d'Aniche. In 1928, he resigned from this position to spend the remainder of his life serving various organizations dedicated to bringing about social and economic reform in France. For his efforts in this field he eventually was named a Chevalier of the Legion of Honor and appointed Minister of Commerce and Industry in the French government in 1953. He was made Minister of Works and Social Security in 1964. He combined his life of political activism with one of scholarly research on the history of political thought and law. The author of a number of essays on these and related subjects, he is best known for his six volume work entitled *La naissance de l'esprit laique au déclin du moyen âge* which appeared from 1934 to 1946.

It is not difficult to notice that Calvinist religious society (the only one which has a semblance of independence in the face of the state), far from being, as some imagine, the "cradle of modern ideas," represented rather a retrogression in respect to the political society that had seen its birth. Calvin did not wish to give his Church even the slightly democratic institutions of sixteenth-century Geneva. In Geneva, the "rabble," so despised by Calvin, directly elected each year the most important magistrates of the city. Calvin did not allow them to play a similar role in the election of the ministers, or even in that of the elders. He did not think it expedient to give the faithful the freedoms that two centuries before Bishop Adhémar Fabri had allowed to his subjects.

One can object, it is true, that in instituting the Council of the Elders, Calvin introduced the representative system into the Church. However timid this regime was, we willingly recognize Calvin's originality on this point. But we do not agree that such a regime (as Calvin conceived of it), introduced anything new in political society. One might believe oneself to be dreaming, when one learns from M. Doumergue, that "authentic Calvinist conceptions" are "at the origin of the representative system." Even if one gives to the role of the community in the Calvinist Church its largest sense, and even if one neglects the important restrictions on it stipulated by Calvin, one still searches in vain for any new principles this conception might have brought to republican Geneva. In what respect did the representation of the Church by the Consistory differ from the representation of the city by the Councils? Only in that in the latter representation was much larger and more influential. All important political questions came before the Council of Two Hundred which did not hesitate to review the decisions of the Syndics. The Consistory, on the contrary, remained under the fist of the ministers. It participated in their government but it did not constitute a representation of the Church which was distinct from its government and destined to control it.

Any unprejudiced mind will agree that Calvin's principles were well behind those which animated the political constitution of Geneva before he preached there.

From Georges de Lagarde, *Recherches sur l'esprit politique de la Réforme* (Paris: A. and J. Picard and Cie, 1926), 66. 453–455. Reprinted by permission of A. and J. Picard and Cie. Translation by Malcolm Sylvers.

Charles Mercier

CALVIN AN UNCONSCIOUS SOURCE OF DEMOCRACY

Charles Mercier (d. 1940) was a native of Belgium but spent most of his life in France. His intense interest in the history, nature, and influence of Calvinist political theory in the sixteenth century was reflected in articles published in the *Revue d'histoire ecclésiastique* and the *Bulletin de la Société de l'histoire du protestantisme français* in 1933 and 1934. He was killed early in World War II.

IF we only consider his political ideas, we are certainly correct that Calvin is not a precursor of modern democracy. In this political philosophy man, considered essentially free and independent, can only be constrained by himself. From this derives the theory of the original sovereignty of the people. Calvin never accepted such a democratic ideology. If he insists in his sermons on the covenant that God has made with his people, this religious contract—if people who possess nothing, not even their free will, are capable of making contracts—is equivalent to a solemn recognition of the rights of God over his faithful subjects, joined to the promise better to serve him, with the help of his grace. Whether it is a question of the origin of society or of the power which directs it, Calvin cannot be, if one keeps only to his political doctrine, considered a precursor of this theory which, breaking with scholastic teaching, opens the way to the political philosophy of the modern era. According to this theory, which is essentially voluntarist, the will of the contractors creates society and is at the origin of all power. If Calvin argues that the institution of the Church is carried out on earth by the constant collaboration (the good will, not the will) of the faithful, he nonetheless maintains that this institution is by its nature anterior to their will. It informs them and dominates them with all the importance of its ends. This "institutionalist" conception of society had been taught by Aristotle and the great scholastics of the Middle Ages. It is equally found at the base of the political conceptions of the author of the *Institutes of the Christian Religion.*

Our conclusions would, however, be incomplete, and thus erroneous, if in this research concerning the influence of Calvin on the development of modern democratic ideas we did not equally take into account his religious doctrine, in which the true political spirit of his Reformation is, in the final analysis, manifest.

We have sufficiently well established that this doctrine is essentially individualist. "To recognize," following Rousseau, "the Bible as the only rule of one's belief, and to admit no other interpreter of the meaning of the Bible than oneself," is truly the foundation of Protestantism. Without a doubt, Calvin thought it possible to bend reason to the authority of the sacred text whose sense, evident in itself, penetrates our soul and carries through our santification under the particular workings of the Holy Spirit. We can already discover an element of human experience and personal determination in this individual inspiration. It will make room, under the influence of Renaissance naturalism and the rationalism which flow from it, for the principle of free examination which itself will clear the way for free thought. If this was neither the doctrine nor the intention of the Reformers it was however the spirit of the Reformation. Given

From Charles Mercier, "L'esprit de Calvin et la démocratie," *Revue d'histoire ecclésiastique* (1934), pp. 50–53. Reprinted by permission of *Revue d'histoire ecclésiastique*. Translation by Malcolm Sylvers.

the essentially individualist orientation that they infused it with, by natural tendency it moved down this way that had been traced for it.

Jean-Jacques Rousseau, himself excommunicated by the Geneva Consistory, wondered, "How had the followers of the Reformation been able to get together on such a principle?" The author of the *Social Contract* discovered in this way, without being aware of it himself, the vice which reappears in his own work, and which is the basic contradiction that undermines the institution of Calvin. "They agreed that they all would recognize each one of them as a competent judge for himself," justly notes the author of the *Letters from the Mountain*. Transposed into the political order, this principle became in Rousseau the basis of the *Social Contract*. It "links the contractors without subjecting them to anyone and in giving them their will alone as a rule, it leaves them as free as before." The entire political doctrine of Rousseau and the democratic ideology which has come out of it rests on this basis. We can see that Rousseau, although rejecting the doctrinal content and the ecclesiastical discipline of the Geneva reformer, nonetheless remains faithful to the spirit which, despite all the energy of Calvin and the strict vigilance of his successors, clearly emanates from the Reformation.

No doubt the contradiction that we have pointed out in Calvin's work between the principle of our private sanctification and the institution of a Church was able to develop later into two contrasting tendencies. By his *Institutes of the Christian Religion,* his ecclesiastical discipline, he inculcated in his disciples, in default of principles of a collective religious life, habits of collaboration and aristocratic self-government. Given certain circumstances and economic conditions, these habits came to reinforce, in a certain measure, among the first emigrants to New England, old Anglo-Saxon political traditions. But it is the first of these two tendencies which dominates.

We willingly agree that this spirit of individualism and independence had already sprung up in Christianity with the naturalism of the Renaissance where everything was brought to the measure of man. But in making of the Christian conscious of his election, the center of religious life, at the same time that he tried to curb him under the yoke of predestination and the Word alone, Calvin shook, without knowing it, the very principle of order. He actually reversed in religion the terms of the essentially subordinate relationship of man to God and thus opened an immense breach through which the spirit of the new era could rush forward. This spirit was that of the independence and of the absolute autonomy of the individual, of which Rousseau has left us the completed form in politics and which we already find in embryonic form in Calvin's *Institutes of the Christian Religion.*

Marc-Edouard Chenevière

CALVIN NOT INTERESTED IN FORMS OF GOVERNMENT

Marc-Edouard Chenevière (b. 1911) has been Editor-in-Chief of *La Suisse,* a leading Genevan daily newspaper, since 1941. He was born in Geneva and received his education there. He earned the degree of "Docteur en droit" at the University of Geneva in 1936. His doctoral dissertation was published as *La pensée politique de Calvin.* His vigorous denial of any direct connection between the political thought of Calvin and the dogmas of modern democracy caused a considerable stir among Calvin scholars throughout the world.

IF the word state means the political organization of a people, the word government designates its form. Until now we have spoken of the necessity of a political organization of society and of the necessary existence of magistrates. But we have not yet spoken of the form that this political organization must take.

We have not yet spoken of it because this problem appears to have little importance for Calvin. For him it is a problem to be solved by empirical reason since Scripture does not speak of it but limits itself to calling for the obedience of Christians toward their rulers, whatever the form of government may be.

Actually, although Calvin in principle admits that one can discuss the question of the best form of government, (and Calvin himself seems to prefer a type of aristocratic regime tempered by democracy) he nonetheless believes that such a discussion, abstractly undertaken without the help of arguments from experience, from history, or simply from circumstances, is of little interest.

In the final analysis, the form of government for Calvin depends strictly on circumstances such as the religious situation found in a given state. And the sympathy or antipathy of Calvin for different forms of government often is dictated more by the religious ends that he is pursuing than by motives of a strictly political order. Calvin is ready to support all governments, whatever be their forms, as long as they favor his religious policy, and above all as long as they have a just comprehension of the role of the state.

This is why, above any personal preference, Calvin demands that one recognize and obey every state, whatever be its form of government, since every state, whatever it be, is willed by God.

It is in the light of this last argument that it is necessary to explain the total indifference that Calvin brings to the problem of the forms of government: "There are many different forms and types of superiors. However they are all the same in this regard, that we must accept them all as ministers ordained by God."

This idea is found in almost all the catechisms and confessions of faith issuing from the Calvinist reformation. The 1537 Confession of Faith proclaims that the domination "equally by kings and princes as by other magistrates and superiors" is something willed by God. All the other official texts of the period are modeled on this one.

Of all the forms of government "the one which is the least pleasing to men is particularly recommended above all others: the *seigneurerie* and domination by a single man which, since it carries with it a common servitude for all—except the one to whose pleasure everyone else is subjected—has never been

From Marc-Edouard Chenevière, *La pensée politique de Calvin* (Geneva and Paris: Labor and Fides, 1937), pp. 181–190. Reprinted by permission of Labor and Fides. Translation by Malcolm Sylvers.

agreeable to men of an excellent and lofty spirit."

This form of government is the more approved by God as it is naturally loved less by men. This is so because every state, whatever be its government, is willed by God, and must consequently be respected.

Since therefore all governments are the work of God, their form matters little because it is necessary to accept them all.

This preoccupation grew proportionately in the different editions of the Calvinist confessions of faith. The one of 1557 speaks of the obedience that must be given to kingdoms and principalities." The one of 1559 adds "kingdom, principality, and *seigneurerie*." That of the churches of France (1559) adds to this list "the republics and all other types of principalities, hereditary or otherwise."

In brief, all forms of government are the work of God: "God has willed that there be men with a superior authority: king, prince or magistrate, according to the varying administrative form of peoples and nations. Because whatever be this public administration, in it gleams a specific gift of God."

This equality is even more significant with regard to the different nuances that can exist within the same form of government: "Kingdoms are limited by the providence of God. Some come through succession and lineage, others are conquered through war by force and sword, still others come by chance. Nonetheless God governs all of them and there is no change in principalities that is not ordered from on high."

It is thus of a secondary interest to discuss abstractly the benefits and inconveniences of the different regimes. "For private men who have no authority to order public things it is certainly a vain pastime to discuss which is the best way to keep order." In his commentary on an epistle of Saint Paul, Calvin adds, "The apostle wished by this word to put an end to the frivolous curiosity of men who are often accustomed to inquiring by what right have those who possess the government of kingdoms and *seigneureries* acquired this power. But it must be enough for us that they are in command, because they did not get there through their own virtue but were put there by the hand of the Lord."

Elsewhere, Calvin states again: "Some are accustomed to inquire too curiously by what right each prince rules. But it must be enough for us to see them govern."

All forms of government are thus equally agreeable in the eyes of God. Consequently the differences which exist between them are of little importance with regard to what they have in common: their foundation in the will of God.

To discuss abstractly the advantages and inconveniences of the different forms of government is absurd since the advantages or inconveniences of each form of government in the final analysis strictly depend on the social circumstances of a given country; "in addition it is reckless simply to weigh these factors since the principal one lies in circumstances." Such a discussion has no practical interest since the peoples do not have the right to change the form of their government by themselves.

Calvin reasons on the subject of governments exactly as he does on the subject of laws.

Provided that a government fulfills the role confided by God to political power, its form is of little concern. Given the changing and diverse nature of the world in which we live, it is even good and necessary that these forms differ according to times and places. There is no more a perfect form of government than there is a positive law perfectly valuable for all times and all countries.

We have already seen a concrete example of the role that Calvin attributes to reason in political science. The role of this faculty is not so much to trace for us *a priori* a perfect system of law or government as it is to draw from the observation of the exterior world the political solutions which seem to be the best: "More than that. If we look not only at one city but consider the entire world and its various countries, we will certainly find that it is by the Providence of God that different regions are governed by different forms of order. Just as the elements can only be kept in good condition by proportion and unequal temperature, so internal order can only be well kept by a certain inequality. To those for whom the will of God is sufficient, it is not necessary to point out everything. If it is His pleasure to place kings in kingdoms and whatever other superiors over free peoples, it is for us to be obedient and subject to whatever superiors rule in the place where we live."

After having thus clearly established the respect that we owe to all forms of government, Calvin then shows that, no matter how seriously undertaken, an abstract discussion will not lead us to any satisfactory solution if it does not take account of the circumstances which favor one or the other of these forms in a given country: "When one compares forms of government without their specific circumstances, it is not easy to tell which would be the most useful since each, at its own level, is almost equal to the others." Such a discussion is only interesting when one compares peoples who are more or less at the same social level.

The 1560 edition of *Institutes of the Christian Religion* brings up the famous classification by Aristotle of the forms of government. Since this reference does not figure in the 1559 edition it is not the work of Calvin himself, but very probably that of the translator. But the latter only expressed what Calvin said in other terms in the 1559 edition when he recalled the three essential forms of government "which the philosophers discuss."

In the 1536 edition Calvin laid out the discussion as follows: after having considered the different forms of government to be equal, he remarked simply that it is very true that a "king or whoever else exercises domination easily becomes a tyrant." But he immediately adds that it "is equally easy when the high-born are in control that they conspire to raise up an unjust domination." These somewhat disillusioned reflections on monarchical and aristocratic regimes do not in any way make Calvin a partisan of the democratic regime. To the contrary, in fact, since he added: "It is even easier when the people have authority that they become seditious."

Such is the position in 1536. In short he closely follows the reasoning of Aristotle and does not come out for any specific form of government. As we have already seen, he believes in the necessity of a certain diversity of the forms of government according to times and places, of the equality of these different forms of government in themselves, if only with regard to the circumstances.

The 1536 text continues in the later editions of 1539 and 1541 which both date from the period when Calvin was in Strasbourg.

In 1543, after he definitively established himself at Geneva, Calvin added the following to the previous text: "If one compares the three forms of government that I have outlined it is true that the most advisable would be that in which those who rule keep the people in freedom." Undoubtedly under the influence of the Geneva constitution that he had just studied and the one of Strasbourg which he had just left, Calvin in 1543 seems to prefer a sort of aristocratic regime tempered by democratic elements.

This inclination of Calvin is still more noticeable if one looks at the Latin text of 1543 rather than the French translation of 1545.

Calvin continues in these terms "because that (the preeminence of the aristocratic regime tempered by democratic elements) has always been approved by experience."

Let us note well how Calvin reasons even when he reasons abstractly. It is experience that must serve as the guide for thought. Calvin persists unconsciously in utilizing experience more than abstract reasoning to find the solution to the problem of government.

However, as we know, experience is not a sufficient criterion and can deceive us. If Calvin seems to prefer the regime we have just spoken of it is because

"God also has confirmed it by his authority when he ordered it for the people of Israel in order to keep them in the best condition possible until He gave them the image of Our Lord Jesus in David. Since the best state of government is that in which there is a well-tempered and long-lasting freedom, therefore, I confess that those who are able to be in such a condition are truly happy and I say they only do their duty if they constantly try to maintain it. Even the rulers of a free people must so apply themselves that the freedom of the people, which they protect, does not diminish at all while in their hands. If they are careless in conserving it or allow it to decay, they are traitors and disloyal. But if those who, by the will of God, live under princes and are their natural subjects, transfer this idea to them and are thus tempted to make a revolt or change, this would be not only mad and useless, but also wicked and pernicious."

Thus, in 1543, Calvin considers that an aristocracy tempered by democracy constitutes the best possible political regime for men: first of all because God has accorded it to his chosen people, but also because experience shows that it is truly so.

Those who live under such a regime should consider themselves happy. All the same, those who live under another regime must support it, because God has wished it so, and not try to overthrow it by revolution. We can see therefore that Calvin's preference is somewhat platonic. The political regime, which one can more exactly style an ideal political regime, is a gift of God. But it is not at all a right which each people can claim and try to achieve for itself. It is good, says Calvin, that certain peoples be brutalized by tyrants; in that case they only receive what they deserve.

In 1559, disgusted no doubt by the policy of the king of France, Calvin seems to oppose, in a new addition to the original text of the *Institutes,* this ideal regime, of which we have just spoken, to the monarchical regime. The superiority of this ideal regime is evident, "not by itself, but because it does not often happen . . . that kings so control themselves that their will never wanders from what is just and right. In addition, it is truly rare that they have sufficient prudence and cleverness that each of them can see what is good and useful. It follows that the vice or defects of men is the reason that the most acceptable and surest form of superiority is that in which several govern helping one another and reminding one another of their duty. If one raises himself too high, the others act as censors and teachers."

But, as Calvin says, an aristocratic regime tempered by democratic elements is not "by itself" superior to the monarchical regime. It is "because it does not often occur" that monarchy escapes degeneration into tyranny. It is therefore experience, and not abstract reasoning which proves that the aristocratic regime is superior to the monarchical one.

Calvin is therefore very logically led to combat the idea of a universal monarchy, since in this case the defects of the monarchical regime would only be accentuated: "Experience shows that the more monarchies expand, the more there is immorality in the world." If a single man is incapable of correctly governing a small state, how could he govern well a large one? One must note that if the medieval ideal of Christendom favored the idea of the universal monarchy, Calvin's entirely different conception of the world led him to reject this same ideal.

It seems, therefore, that for reasons of personal experience coupled with biblical motives, Calvin, just as Zwingli and perhaps even Luther, saw the ideal political regime as aristocratic.

There is nothing astonishing in this. Calvin begins with the idea that society is a whole and not the result of a social contract. The doctrines of natural individual rights or of popular sovereignty have no meaning for him. Society is a given totality which God wishes to conduct to its best end. It is entirely natural that he does not choose for this end a single man, since we are aware of the excesses which often occur in monarchies. It is no less natural that he does not give all the power to the people. Calvin knows very well that one cannot have confidence in the wisdom of the people.

It is therefore perfectly logical that Calvin gives his preference to an aristocratic regime in which the reins of government are, theoretically, in the hands of the best. It is possible that the Calvinist doctrine of predestination is not extraneous to this preference. However, Calvin is well aware that one cannot have an absolute confidence, even in a government of the best. This is why he thinks that the people, for the good of which God has truly constituted political regimes, must have its say in the political life of the country. If therefore Calvin mixes democratic elements with aristocratic constitutions, he nevertheless remains completely foreign to the dogmas of modern democracy. As we have already seen, he does not believe either in popular sovereignty or in individual rights. The participation of the people in the life of the state is for him only a means through which the political machine can be made to run. It is not at all a right which belongs to the people in every case. "Such a freedom is a special gift and, in fact, we see that it is not at all given to everyone." Calvin knows perfectly that the active participation of the people in public life is often harmful to the good progress of the state.

There is therefore, in one sense, an ideal political regime. But this political regime is only truly ideal if the people have acquired a sufficient political maturity; without that an authoritarian regime is preferable. In an absolute sense there is no ideal political regime. There are only regimes which are more or less good according to the circumstances.

Winthrop S. Hudson

CALVIN A SOURCE OF RESISTANCE THEORY, AND THEREFORE OF DEMOCRACY

Winthrop S. Hudson (b. 1911) has been for some time one of the leading church historians in the United States. He earned his B.A., B.D., and Ph.D. degrees at Kalamazoo College, Colgate Rochester Divinity School, and the University of Chicago respectively. He taught, in turn, at the latter two institutions before finally returning to Colgate Rochester Divinity School in 1947, where he is now Professor of Church History. Hudson is the author of many articles and books on the Reformation and on the history of American Christianity. He currently serves on the Council of both the American Society of Church History and the American Baptist Historical Society and is a past president of both organizations.

DURING recent years there has been an interesting shift in the attitude of many historians with regard to the relationship of Calvinism to the development of democracy. A generation ago, the contention that modern democracy was a daughter of Calvinism was eminently respectable in academic circles.

From Winthrop S. Hudson, "Democratic Freedom and Religious Faith in the Reformed Tradition," *Church History*, XV (1946), 177–194. Reprinted by permission of *Church History* and courtesy of the author.

The fact that modern democracy arose and put down its strongest roots in lands most deeply influenced by the Reformed faith—in England, Scotland, Holland, America and Switzerland—was regarded as self-evident confirmation of this contention.

Within the present generation this thesis as to the relationship of Calvinism and democracy has been sharply challenged. The development of democracy in Calvinist countries is said to be an historical accident, and the forces which produced the democratic patterns of government are said to have been social and economic rather than religious. If ideological parentage is to be sought, it is asserted, it will be found in the essentially secular philosophies of the English Levellers and Deists rather than among the Calvinists. The Calvinists, far from fostering democratic ideas, resisted them. Their ideal was the aristocratic ideal expressed in the lines of Nathaniel Ward:

> The upper world shall rule
> While stars will run their race;
> The nether world obey
> While people keep their place.

The interest of the Calvinists was in the establishment of a theocracy governed by the elect, and their true sentiments are revealed in the words of such men as John Winthrop and John Cotton. "A democracy," said Winthrop, "is, among most civil nations, accounted the meanest and worst of all forms of government." "Democracy?" Cotton asked rhetorically. "I do not conceive that ever God did ordain it as a fit government either for church or commonwealth."

Marc-Edouard Chenevière is, perhaps, the best spokesman for the newer point of view. In *La pensée politique de Calvin* (1937), he points out that to regard Calvin as the spiritual parent of democracy, it is necessary to consider Beza, Hotman, Mornay, William of Orange, Buchanan, Althusius, and Roger Williams as the true representatives of Calvinism. But, he continues, these men are not orthodox Calvinists, and to the extent that they defended liberal and democratic ideas they merely developed ideas arising before the Reformation in the "full" Middle Ages, and even these ideas were not democratic in the modern sense of the term. Furthermore, these men do not merit the title of Calvinist political theorists because they were far more preoccupied with meeting the immediate political needs of their coreligionists than with seeking, as did Calvin, to trace the fundamental principles of a political doctrine inspired by the Word of God. This is made clear, he asserts, when one notes that the infinite variations of the political doctrines of these men follow the needs of the moment and affect, not merely the application, but the fundamental principles of Calvin's thought. It is true, of course, that the Reformation indirectly favored the development of democratic ideas by the creation of religious minorities in a number of countries, but this fact scarcely makes the Reformers the spiritual parents of modern democracy.

The central contention, then, is this: the Calvinists by creating religious minorities in certain countries prepared the way for democracy, but there was no rational basis for such a development in their thought. The inherent logic of their doctrines would not demand such a result, nor even make it possible without seriously compromising their principles. The development of democracy was at best an unintentional result. By throwing themselves into opposition to existing regimes, the Calvinists cultivated an atmosphere and a sentiment which was congenial to democratic ideas and actually stimulated their development, but the end they sought was not rule by the people. Indeed, they created a situation which made impossible the solution they desired—the aristocratic rule of the elect. Nor was the opposition to the existing regimes due primarily to inherent political principles in Calvinistic thought, but rather to the fact that the Reformed groups found themselves compelled to struggle for existence in a hostile environment. Forced to demand rights for themselves, they found it difficult and ultimately impossible to deny them to others.

This reconstruction contains large elements of truth but the overall conclusion is both false and misleading. Roland H. Bainton has said with reference to the development of religious freedom: "If Calvin ever wrote anything in favor of religious liberty it was a typographical error." To make a similar sweeping statement with regard to Calvin and democracy would be unjust and untrue. An examination of the literature of Calvinism, I believe, will disclose four basic propositions which should govern our thinking in this area.

1. It is a mistake to identify Calvinism with a small group of New England oligarchs as if they were representative of the movement as a whole. Not only is this to ignore Ponet, Goodman, Knox, Beza, Hotman, Mornay, William of Orange, Althusius, and a good many others who certainly stood in the Reformed tradition; it is to substitute what became a minor current for the major stream.
2. It is a mistake to regard Calvinism as a static body of political dogma. The contribution of Calvinism in the seventeenth and eighteenth centuries cannot be measured by what Calvin said in 1536. A movement can never be identified with a certain body of rigid and unchanging principles, for that would be to deny the historical process itself. A movement can only be described and identified in terms of a continuity which maintains a degree of inner consistency. We can trace considerable change in Calvin's thought from 1536 to 1559, and yet in that development Calvin did not involve himself in any fundamental contradictions.
3. The thought of Calvin provided the potential basis for the elaboration of democratic ideas. Not only did he provide a basis for resistance to the exercise of arbitrary power, but his thought did not preclude the formulation of a definitely democratic philosophy of government. The assumption that the Calvinist ideal involved, of necessity, government by the elect is simply a fiction.
4. These democratic ideas were in fact elaborated by Calvinists.

Basic to any real understanding of the influence of Calvinism in the development of democracy is the recognition of Calvin's active and profound interest in politics. "Calvinism," declares V. H. Rutgers, "has never manifested indifference with regard to the state." On the contrary, Calvinism has always regarded the state as a positive good, and politics as a legitimate and even an obligatory concern of the religious man.

Calvin explicitly rejected the concept prevalent in some Protestant circles that since the world is evil, one must refrain from participation in the activities of the world, which meant specifically that one must refrain from participation in the activities of government. With equal definiteness, Calvin rejected the view that the state was a mere concession to sin which must be tolerated and in the activities of which one must participate only as a citizen and not as a Christian. Civil government, he affirmed, is not "a polluted thing, which has nothing to do with Christian men" (*Institutes,* IV, xx, 2). It is a "benevolent provision" of God through which he effects his purposes. It is not simply a remedy for evil, a restraint for sin, a consequence of the fall; it is a positive good. Government makes possible the right ordering of life which is necessary to all communal living, and "is equally as necessary to mankind as bread and water, light and air, and far more excellent." For it enables men "to secure the accommodations arising from all these things" and "enables them to live together" (*Institutes,* IV, xx, 3). An even more important end of government, however, is to glorify God by creating a holy community. The state is an instrument in the hands of God by which he effects his will. Politics, therefore, is the concern of the Christian as a Christian, and not simply as a citizen in an evil world. The will of God is supreme and must be obeyed not merely in the individual life but in the collective life as well. The community must be Christianized and the world brought into harmony with the divine will.

At this point we become involved in one of the apparent paradoxes of Calvinist thought. Calvin pictured God "not as idly beholding from heaven the transactions which happened in the world, but as holding the helm of the universe and regulating all events," even the most minute. And yet Calvin constantly emphasized the duties and obligations of men to effect God's will in the world. With regard to political matters, on the one hand, it is God, irrespective of human desires and efforts, who effects his will through the state; on the other hand, it is the duty of those who are involved in the affairs of state to effect the purposes of God. The paradox, of course, is more apparent than real, and can be be resolved by letting Calvin speak for himself.

> He who has fixed the limits of our life, has also intrusted us with the care of it; has furnished us with means and supplies for its preservation; has also made us provident of dangers; and, that they may not oppress us unawares, has furnished us with cautions and remedies. Now, it is evident what is our duty. If God has committed to us the preservation of our life, we should preserve it; if he offers supplies, we should use them; if he forewarns us of dangers, we should not rashly run into them; if he furnishes remedies, we ought not to neglect them. But it will be objected, no danger can hurt, unless it has been ordained that it shall hurt us, and then no remedies can avert it. But what if dangers are therefore not fatal, because God has assigned you remedies to repulse and overcome them? . . . You conclude that it is unnecessary to guard against danger because, if it be not fatal, we shall escape it without caution; but, on the contrary, the Lord enjoins you to use caution, because he intends it not to be fatal to you . . . The arts of deliberation and caution in men proceed from the inspiration of God, and . . . subserve the designs of his providence in the preservation of their lives; as, on the contrary, by neglect and slothfulness, they procure to themselves the evils which he has appointed for them . . . It has pleased God to conceal from us all future events, that we may meet them as doubtful contingenies, and not cease to oppose to them the remedies with which we are provided, till they shall have been surmounted, or shall have overcome all our diligence (*Insti.*, I, xvii, 4).

The effect of Calvinistic thinking, therefore, was not to lessen the sense of individual responsibility, but actually to increase it. The political order was of concern to the Christian man, and he was expected to shape it into a holy commonwealth with whatever means God had provided.

In assessing the influence of Calvinism in the development of modern democracy, we must give our attention, first of all, to the twin pillars upon which democracy rests: (1) the idea of limited sovereignty, of a government under law, of limits beyond which government cannot go and to which it must conform; (2) the right of resistance when these limits arc exceeded. These two concepts do not constitute the length and breadth of democracy, but they are the foundation stones upon which democracy rests. . . .

Calvin's fundamental postulate was the absolute sovereignty of God, and in the realm of politics that meant that God was the "King of kings" to whose will the desires of earthly princes must be subject, to whose decrees their commands must yield, to whose majesty their sceptres must submit (*Insti.*, IV, xx, 32). As the vice-regents of God, princes were obliged to "exhibit to men an image, as it were, of the providence, care, goodness, benevolence, and justice of God" (*Insti.*, IV, xx, 6). Magistrates, therefore, are limited in the exercise of their power by the superior authority of God, and their rule must ever be in subjection to the precepts of natural law as made manifest in the Scriptures. "The written law (of Scripture)," Calvin said, "is just an attestation of the law of nature, through means of which God recalls to our memory that which he has previously engraved on our hearts" (*Comm. on Psalms* 119:52).

Within the Scriptures, Calvin distinguishes between ceremonial, judicial, and moral law. The first two have no abiding authority. They are variable, apply only to a specific time and place, and find their validation solely as they conform to the dictates of the moral law which is eternal and forever binding.

> The moral law is comprised in two leading articles, of which one simply commands us to worship God with pure faith

and piety, and the other enjoins us to embrace men with sincere love,—this law, I say, is the true and eternal rule of righteousness, prescribed to men of all ages and nations, who wish to conform their lives to the will of God. For this is his eternal and immutable will, that he himself be worshipped by us all, and that we mutually love one another . . . These judicial regulations, though they had no other end than the preservation of that love, which is enjoined in the eternal law of God, yet had something which distinguished them from the precept itself. As the ceremonies, therefore, might be abrogated without any violation or injury of piety, so the precepts and duties of love remain of perpetual obligation, notwithstanding the abolition of all these judicial ordinances . . . All nations are left at liberty to enact such laws as they shall find to be respectively expedient for them; provided they be framed according to that perpetual rule of love (*Insti.*, IV, xx, 15).

The moral law is not a mere arbitrary divine requirement. Its purpose, among other things, is to secure the well being of mankind, and the purpose of government is to make it effective in the world. The vocation of magistrates, therefore, is "not to rule for their own interest, but for the public good." Magistrates are "ordained by God for the well being of mankind." Consequently, they are not "endued with unbridled power, but what is restricted to the well being of their subjects, in short they are responsible to God and to men in the exercise of their power" (*Comm. on Romans* 13:3–4).

It is the moral law, then, which serves as a "bridle" to the governing power, and Calvin suggests that the judicial law which implements it should be reduced to writing so that "recourse may be had to the written law" and "the mutual obligation of head and members" may be apparent to all. Especially to be preferred is a covenant or compact, such as a coronation oath, by which "kings and princes pledge their faith to the people."

The idea that magistrates were limited and bound by the requirements of natural law was not a novel idea in the sixteenth century. It had been axiomatic throughout the period of the Middle Ages, but two novel elements were introduced into the general orthodox political thought of the period by the Protestant Reformers. The first was a general Protestant contribution which involved the affirmation of the competence of the individual to judge for himself when a ruler was subverting the ends for which he had been ordained and had become a tyrant. The second was more definitely a contribution of Reformed thought and involved the elaboration of constitutional means by which the people might resist the encroachments of tyranny.

Ernest Barker has asserted that "St. Thomas Aquinas—like the clerical thinkers of the Middle Ages in general —is a Whig; he believes in popular sovereignty, popular institution of monarchy, a pact between king and people, and the general tenets of Locke." Barker fails to mention, however, that between the king and the people stood the church, and that it was the church which determined when the rights of the people had been subverted. It was the responsibility of the pope "to judge and punish Emperors or Kings, to receive complaints against them, to shield nations from their tyranny, and to discharge their subjects from the oath of fealty." Unfortunately the church did not prove to be a very efficient guardian of the liberties of the people. It was unable to bring to a halt the progressive concentration of power that was taking place throughout Europe, and it failed to prevent the emergence of authoritarian regimes. The national states, perhaps, had become too strong to be easily amenable to ecclesiastical censure, and the church was beset by the perennial temptation of an institution to arrive as a *modus vivendi* with competing authorities in order to preserve its own institutional prerogatives and privileges. In any event the church as an institution did not fulfill its role as the protector of the people against the abuse of civil power.

A principal effect of the Reformation was to make the people once again the judges of their own liberties under God. By denying the authority of the Roman church, the possibility of an appeal to Rome as a defense against tyranny was eliminated, and by emphasizing the right of individual judgment, a foundation was laid for an appeal to the people. The Bible, of course, was the supreme touchstone by which the conduct of a ruler was to be tried, and the practical consequence of the Reformation was to place the interpretation of the Bible in the hands of the individual believer.

This incipient basis for resistance was not elaborated in Lutheranism for two reasons: (1) the issue was not raised in any acute form due to the generally favorable circumstances in which Lutheranism arose; (2) Lutheranism manifested little interest in the temporal affairs of the world. From Luther's point of view, not too much could or should be expected of earthly rulers. All men, to a greater or lesser degree, are slaves to sin and the temporal life is, therefore, destined to be an evil estate. The most that can reasonably be required of the governing power is that it should restrain men from the more flagrant and socially dangerous outcomes of their evil desires, and that the liberty of the church to proclaim the gospel should be preserved and protected.

Calvin, on the other hand, was deeply concerned with political arrangements and was convinced that the state had a positive role to play. The very "image of God ought to be conspicuous in a magistrate" (*Insti.*, IV, xx, 24), and it was his duty not simply to restrain men from the more flagrant sins, but actually his duty embraced the creation of a holy commonwealth. In Calvinism, then, the magistrate was subjected to a much more extensive, inclusive and rigid standard of judgment. Much more was to be expected of him.

While the individual might clearly judge as to whether or not a ruler was a tyrant, it was not necessarily the vocation of every individual to resist tyranny. Magistrates are ordained by God and as such are entitled to honor and obedience. "It is impossible," said Calvin, "to resist the magistrate without, at the same time, resisting God himself" (*Insti.*, IV, xx, 23), and this is true even of the worst of magistrates. The "authority of magistrates . . . is entitled to the greatest veneration. . . . , even though it reside in those who are most unworthy of it, and who, as far as in them lies, pollute it by their iniquity" (*Insti.*, IV, xx, 31).

A man of the worst character, and most undeserving of all honour, who holds the sovereign power, really possesses that eminent and divine authority, which the Lord has given by his word to the ministers of his justice and judgment; and, therefore, . . . he ought to be regarded by his subjects, as far as pertains to public obedience, with the same reverence and esteem which they would show to the best of kings (*Insti.*, IV, xx, 25).

Quite obviously, it is not within the province of a private person to seek to remedy the evils of tyranny (*Insti.*, IV, xx, 29). "Private persons ought . . . not, without being called upon, (to) intermeddle with affairs of state, or rashly intrude themselves into the office of magistrates, or undertake anything of a public nature" (*Insti.*, IV, xx, 31). A private person's only recourse is "to implore the aid of the Lord, in whose hand are the hearts of kings and the revolutions of kingdoms" (*Insti.*, IV, xx, 31), and who will ultimately break the sceptres of insolent kings and overthrow tyrannical governments.

Calvin's counsel of unlimited and unqualified obedience is rather deceptive and provides G. P. Gooch with the basis for his charge that Calvin indulged in political double-talk. Calvin does seem to be advocating absolute and unconditional submission to authority, regardless of its character. In a pure monarchy this would be true, for in a pure monarchy the king alone possesses a public vocation. But not only did Calvin consider a pure monarchy undesirable, he was quite certain that no such form of government existed in Europe. Consequently, the discussion of rights and duties and obligations under a monarchy was academic and irrelevant. The governments of Europe were mixed governments and they provided certain constitutional means of resistance. The passage in which this is stated is crucial and should be quoted in full.

> Although the Lord takes vengeance on unbridled domination, let us not therefore suppose that that vengeance has been committed to us, to whom no command has been given but to obey and suffer. I speak only of private men. For when popular magistrates have been appointed to curb the tyranny of kings (as the Ephori, who were opposed to kings among the Spartans, or Tribunes of the people to consuls among the Romans, or Demarchs to the senate among the Athenians; and perhaps there is something similar to this in the power exercised in each kingdom by the three orders, when they hold their primary diets), so far am I from forbidding these officially to check the undue license of kings, that if they connive at kings when they tyrannise and insult over the humbler of the people, I affirm that their dissimulation is not free from nefarious perfidy, because they fraudulently betray the liberty of the people, while knowing that, by the ordinance of God, they are its appointed guardians (*Insti.*, IV, xx, 31).

Those who have been "appointed guardians" of "the liberty of the people," Calvin says, not only may but must resist and oppose the encroachments of tyranny.

Calvin felt that the best government was a mixture of aristocracy and democracy, such as prevailed in Geneva, where the "people" have a public vocation, and where the people "act in perfect consistence with their duty" when "they exert their strenuous and constant efforts for its preservation" (*Insti.*, IV, xx, 8). Some governments, however, were a mixture of monarchy and aristocracy, and in them a public vocation was confined to the inferior magistrates. In such a state the people are not "to take the business into their own hands" when something in the "public administration" requires correction. "I mean," Calvin continues, "that they ought to attempt nothing without being commanded; for when they have the command of a governor, then they also are invested with public authority" (*Insti.*, IV, xx, 23). That is to say, the people, even in a state where they have no public vocation, may take action to correct abuses of power under the leadership of the inferior magistrates.

Calvin did not define the role of the inferior magistrates, nor did he describe the manner in which they were to exercise their vocation as guardians of the liberties of the realm, but his disciples did. . . .

Men of the sixteenth and seventeenth centuries were well aware of the anti-absolutist temper of Calvinist thinking, and they had no doubts as to the source of what some of them called the rebellious and seditious notions of the time. Richard Bancroft, chaplain to Elizabeth's archbishop of Canterbury and soon to be archbishop himself, pointed an accusing finger at Geneva and documented the charge in his book, *Dangerous Positions and Proceedings* (1593). James I echoed the accusation at the Hampton Court Conference, and after the Restoration, in 1663, Robert South repeated the charge. "In our account of the sons of Geneva," he said, "we will begin with the father of the faithful; faithful, I mean, to their old antimonarchical doctrines and assertions; that is, the great mufti of Geneva"—John Calvin.

The concepts of limited sovereignty and the right of resistance may be the necessary foundation stones for the erection of a democratic philosophy, but taken by themselves they scarcely can be regarded as constituting a democratic philosophy. Calvinism, to be sure, did ultimately come to terms with democratic thought and actually fostered its development, but there are two crucial questions in estimating the influence of Calvinism in this development. (1) Were these tendencies toward democracy present in Calvin's own thinking? (2) Did their fulfillment involve Calvinism in any fundamental contradictions with reference to its basic theological structure?

Theoretically Calvin was indifferent to the three classically defined forms of government—monarchy, aristocracy, and democracy. A godly commonwealth could exist under any of the three forms, and all three could easily be perverted. "The transition," he said, "is easy from monarchy to despotism; it is not much more difficult from aristocracy to oligarchy . . . . ; but it is most easy of all from democracy to sedition" (*Inst.*, IV, xx, 8).

Monarchy, which he defined as "the dominion of one person, whether called a king, or a duke, or any other title," Calvin utterly misliked. "It very rarely happens," he observed, "that kings regulate themselves so that their will is never at variance with justice and rectitude," nor are they "endued with such penetration and prudence, as in all cases to discover what is best" (*Insti.*, IV, xx, 8). A monarchy possesses no provision for restraining the arrogance and ambition of the king, and this to Calvin was its major defect. Few Calvinists, however, were ever willing to admit that a pure monarchy existed, and many of them, following the logic of Calvin's thought, insisted that one could not exist. It was inconceivable to them that, on the basis of natural (or moral) law, God could ordain or the people could consent to a government which made no provision for bridling the rapacity of a would be tyrant.

Calvin's convictions as to what constituted the most desirable form of government underwent progressive change during the years. In the first edition of the *Institutes,* written before his arrival in Geneva, aristocracy had his preference. After seven years experience in the Swiss city, he favored "either aristocracy or a mixture of aristocracy and democracy" such as was practiced in Geneva. Sixteen years later, in the 1559 edition of the *Institutes,* he stresses the fact that it is "safer and more tolerable for the government to be in the hands of many, that they may afford each other mutual assistance and admonition, and that if any one arrogate to himself more than is right, the many may act as censors and masters to restrain his ambition." "No kind of government is more happy than this . . . , and I consider those as the most happy people, who are permitted to enjoy such a condition," in which they have the right and duty to "exert their strenuous and constant efforts" to preserve their liberties.

This "mixture of aristocracy and democracy" was, of course, the form of government advocated by the leaders of the American Revolution, and it was this form of government which was adopted in the Constitution of 1789. Instead of a "mixed state," we now call it a representative democracy, but it possesses all the features of a mixture of aristocracy and democracy. The judges, guardians of the liberties of the people, are appointed for life. The executive originally was intended to be (and still is theoretically) chosen by a council of the "wisest heads" of the nation, and he in turn, with the advice and consent of the Senate, appoints the chief officers of the state. The legislative power does not rest with the people but is exercised by a bi-cameral body, the upper portion of which was originally not elected by a direct vote of the people. No provision has yet been made for popular initiative and referendum. And, finally, both the executive and the legislators are elected for definite terms and are not subject to recall. In the post-Revolutionary period, Hamilton laid more stress on the aristocratic element in the federal government, while Jefferson emphasized the democratic element, but neither denied its essential mixed character. Even the term "democratic republican," which Jefferson adopted as his party label, was an affirmation of the "mixed state" ideal. John Adams, who certainly ought to have known what was in the minds of the early leaders, explicitly acknowledged the debt which the "founding fathers" owed to Calvin and the political theorists of Calvinism.

The major obstacle to a frank recognition of this debt is the fact that the Calvinist theological system, to many modern interpreters, seems antithetical to a democratic philosophy of government. The acceptance of democracy by a Calvinist seems to involve Calvinism in at least two fundamental contradictions.

One of these apparent contradictions is the major burden of Marc-Edouard Chenevière's *La Pensée Politique de*

Calvin (1937). He states his contention in these words:

> Calvin was a determined adversary of modern democracy, that is to say of the political doctrine which makes the people the only legitimate and possible holder of power and sovereignty. For Calvin, God is the sole sovereign; to God alone belongs the power; he is able to delegate it to whom he wishes, to one man as well as to several men or to all the people together, depending upon the circumstances and political maturity of each people. But in no case does Calvin admit that the people are the sovereign from which emanates all power. The people are one of the instruments which God is able to use in order to organize political life in a given country, but they are nothing more (10).
>
> How could Calvin speak of the sovereignty of the people, when he believed only in the sovereignty of God and recognized in the world only the powers delegated by God? For him, the people are only one instrument among others, to which God had given some powers, but to which power in general did not belong. (325).

The major current of Calvinism, beginning with Ponet, Goodman, Hotman, Mornay, and other contemporaries of Calvin, solved this problem in the same way in which many earlier political theorists had solved it. They assumed that God delegated his powers to the people before delegating them to the magistrates, and that, therefore, the people were in a position superior to that of the magistrate. Although the power was derived from God, the people were given the determining voice as to the manner in which the power should be exercised—that is to say, ultimate sovereignty may reside in God but it is mediated through the people. The actual powers of government, qualified, to be sure, by divine requirements, rest upon the consent of the governed. This type of thinking would have been congenial to the mature Calvin, and Christopher Goodman stated that it had his specific approval. Calvin, he said, thought that the propositions contained in his *Superior Powers* (1559) were "somewhat harsh" with regard to the reigning monarchs and should, therefore, be "handled with caution," but "he nevertheless admitted them to be true."

There is a sense, however, even in modern democratic thought, in which we may affirm the sovereignty of God above that of the people. To the extent that we believe that there are certain unalienable rights, belonging to all people everywhere, which cannot be abridged or destroyed by the democratic process, there is an area in which God is sovereign over and beyond any action of the people.

Chenevière feels that an attempt to reconcile democratic theory with a conception of the sovereignty of God involves a second difficulty. The magistrate, he says, as the representative of God cannot be the representative of the people. Once again, this is to create a problem that did not exist in the mind of Calvin. As the representative of God the magistrate is the representative of the people. The interests of God and the people are not separate but parallel. It is the divine intention that magistrates shall devote themselves to the public good and shall be restricted in their activities to the well being of their subjects. "They are," therefore, "responsible to God and to men in the exercise of their power" (*Comm. on Romans* 13:3–4).

What has troubled modern interpreters of the political aspect of Calvinism more than anything else, however, has been the assumption that the theocratic character of the Calvinist ideal necessitates government by the elect. This they find difficult to reconcile with government by the people. Consequently they find it impossible to conceive of Calvinism coming to terms with democracy without doing violence to the Calvinist ideal itself. The dilemma, fortunately, is more apparent than real, for the assumption that government by the elect is inherent in the Calvinist ideal is false.

It is to misunderstand Calvinism completely to think that God is limited to the saints as instruments through which he accomplishes his ends in the world. The reprobate are equally servants of his will. Furthermore, a distinction must be made between the doctrine of special grace and the doctrine of common grace, between the spirit of sanctification which believers alone possess and the operation of the spirit in all creatures. God has not abandoned his creation to the destructive effects of sin. He is ever intervening by common grace or providence to save the creation and to effect his purposes in the world. It is this concept of common grace which provides a foundation for a democratic philosophy.

To contend that early Calvinism anticipated and elaborated all the elements of modern democracy would be utterly naive and far from the truth. Many of the items which now seem an integral part of our democratic heritage—techniques of representation, party organization, provision for the role of the opposition, guarantee of minority rights, universal public education—were the result of a long process of germination, growth and maturation. They did not burst into bloom at once. They were the product of the growing experience and practical necessities of a developing historical movement. Freedom of conscience, freedom of the press, freedom of assembly, and freedom from arbitrary judicial procedures were discovered to be imperative if democracy was to function. The same is true of the organizational aspects of the modern democratic state. They are the product of democratic life rather than the producers of it.

The fact that these elements of modern democracy were not elaborated by Calvin in 1536 or 1559 does not constitute a denial of parentage. A bud does not have all the characteristics of a full-blown flower, a child does not have all the qualities of an adult, an egg does not even resemble a chicken—but the relationship between them all is direct and intimate. While early Calvinism did not possess all the characteristics of modern democracy, nevertheless it has played an important role in its development. The relationship has been intimate and direct.

II. DID CALVIN AND HIS FOLLOWERS FAVOR DEMOCRACY AS A FORM OF GOVERNMENT?

Aristotle and Cicero

CLASSICAL DEFINITIONS OF THE FORMS OF GOVERNMENT

Aristotle (384–322 B.C.) of Ancient Greece and Cicero (106–43 B.C.) of Ancient Rome are two of the great seminal political thinkers of Western Civilization. Aristotle was a professional philosopher and, after 335 B.C., the master of the most famous educational institution of his day, the Lyceum. The first of the following brief passages is from his famous *Politics*. In that work he not only analyzed the forms of government but also expounded upon the origin and nature of the state, revolution, and *The Republic* of his famous teacher, Plato. Like most educated Romans of his time, Cicero owed his philosophical outlook as much to Plato and Aristotle as to Stoicism. But unlike Plato and Aristotle, he was less a political theorist and more a practicing politician. He became the leading lawyer of his era and held the highest offices of the Roman state. The following excerpt from his *Republic* contains his classic defense of mixed government. Both Aristotle and Cicero were widely read by Calvin and most of the other major thinkers of the sixteenth and seventeenth centuries.

THE government, which is the supreme authority in states, must be in the hands of one, or of a few, or of many. The true forms of government, therefore, are those in which the one, or the few, or the many, govern with a view to the common interest; but governments which rule with a view to the private interest, whether of the one, or of the few, or of the many, are perversions. For citizens, if they are truly citizens, ought to participate in the advantages of a state. Of forms of government in which one rules, we call that which regards the common interests, kingship or royalty; that in which more than one, but not many, rule, aristocracy [the rule of the best]; and it is so called, either because the rulers are the best men, or because they have at heart the best interests of the state and of the citizens. But when the citizens at large administer the state for the common interest, the government is called by the generic name,—a polity. And there is a reason for this use of language. One man or a few may excel in virtue; but of virtue there are many kinds: and as the number increases it becomes more difficult for them to attain perfection in every kind, though they may in military virtue, for this is found in the masses. Hence, in a polity the fighting-men have the supreme power, and those who possess arms are the citizens.

Of the above-mentioned forms, the perversions are as follows:—of royalty, tyranny; or aristocracy, oligarchy; of polity, democracy. For tyranny is a kind of monarchy which has in view the interest of the monarch only; oligarchy has in view the interest of the wealthy; democracy, of the needy: none of them the common good of all.

Laelius: But of the three simple forms of state, Scipio, which do you especially approve?

Scipio: You frame your question well when you ask, "Which of the three" I especially approve, because I do not approve any one of them considered separately and by itself. I prefer rather the mixed form, which is a combination of all three, to any one taken by itself. Still, if I had to express preference for one of the unmixed forms, I should choose monarchy and accord it first place. In this kind of state we find that the king is described as if he were a father, planning for his subjects as if they were his children, and zealously protecting them but never reducing them to subjection. Thus it is much better for the weak and ignorant to be guarded by the care of one man, who is at once the strongest and the best man in the state. There are, to be sure, the aristocrats, who claim that they do this better than the king, and assert that there would be greater wisdom in a number of men than in one, and withal the same justice and good faith. Finally, the people themselves declare loudly that they do not wish to obey either one man or several. Nothing, they say, is sweeter than freedom, even to wild beasts; and no citizen possesses freedom when he is subject either to a king or to an aristocracy.

Thus I prefer monarchy for the love which the king bears to his subjects; aristocracy for its wisdom in counsel; and democracy for its freedom. When I compare them, I find it hard to decide which feature we desire the most.

From George H. Sabine and Stanley B. Smith, eds., *On the Commonwealth: Marcus Tullius Cicero* (Columbus, Ohio: Ohio State University Press, 1929), p. 140. Reprinted with the permission of the Bobbs-Merrill Co. Inc.

Josef Bohatec

CALVIN PREFERRED EITHER ARISTOCRACY OR A MIXTURE OF ARISTOCRACY AND DEMOCRACY

Josef Bohatec (1876–1954) was born in Kochow in Moravia in what was then the Austrian Empire. Serving for more than forty years on the Protestant Theological Faculty of the University of Vienna, he became one of the leading twentieth-century authorities on Calvin and Calvinism. He was the author of scores of articles and books on Calvinist religious and political thought. Many scholars feel that his *Calvins Lehre von Staat und Kirche,* published in 1937, is the most profound work on the Genevan reformer's political thought yet written. Others, such as Hans Baron and John T. McNeill, reject his attempt to minimize Calvin's contribution to the development of modern democratic concepts and make his political thought dependent upon ancient philosophy, particularly on a so-called Aristotelian "organic pneumato-cratical principle."

As an ideal form Calvin wavers between aristocracy and a mixed form of aristocracy and democracy. Despite this obvious fact, there persist among Calvin scholars assertions which depict Calvin as favoring either a pure democracy or a pure aristocracy and correspondingly speak of a democratic or aris-

From Josef Bohatec, *Calvins Lehre von Staat und Kirche* (Breslau: Marcus Verlag, 1937), pp. 124–128, 158–164. Reprinted with permission of Schilling Und Co. and Theodor Marcus. Translation by Jonathan Wagner and Robert D. Linder.

tocratic principle in him. As a result important cultural-historical inferences develop from a generally unproven assumption, from the belief that Calvin's church, "the patroness of civil and political society was strictly democratic." The current of democratic freedom, it is maintained, flowed into the modern world in three forceful streams, the French Calvinist, the English Calvinist, and the American Calvinist. In so doing, Calvinism saved Europe and European democracy. At the other extreme another group of scholars believe that it is impossible to find anything democratic about the Picard reformer. They hold that what he represented was pure aristocracy.

Also there is no lack of those who place Calvin in a middle position between both extremes. To be sure, they admit that the personal views of the reformer were as undemocratic and authoritarian as possible. Nevertheless, they contend that the involvement of a community church with a city republic worked strongly to develop both democratic thinking and the principle of the people's sovereignty. Finally, there are others who wish to solve the problem by attributing to Calvinism and not Calvin a predisposition toward democracy.

This noteworthy conflict of opinions is attributable to the fact that research, in dealing with the constitutional significance of Calvin's democratic principles, fails to place sufficient emphasis upon his statements concerning the two political systems which together he designates as ideal. At the same time, however, it makes them the foundations of its examination. Yet, the dual determination of the ideal form cannot be ignored. Therefore, in the attempt to interpret the democratic system as the only ideal form from the homiletic writings, one seeks to brush aside any difficulties by assuming that the difference between the *Institutes* and the sermons rests on a natural emphasis which is not necessarily a contradiction. This is a well-known subterfuge which seems thoroughly illusory because of the aristocratic thought patterns appearing in the sermons.

On the other hand, there are those who hold that Calvin in no way could have regarded only the aristocratic system as valid. This same school of thought accepts the aristocratic character of the constitution created in Geneva by Calvin, or at least with his substantial participation. Yet, in so doing they neglect to establish the measure of that participation. More specifically, they fail to inquire as to what extent the aristocratic components had already existed before the reorganization by Calvin and his assistants. However, it is possible for others to arrive at the conviction that Calvin's strengthening of the aristocratic elements rests upon a misunderstanding of the real circumstances. They then would find it necessary to ascertain a conflict between the aristocratic theory and the democratic practice, that is the democratic public spirit of the reformer.

Calvin's activism, which comes to light in his striving to reconcile theory with practice, warns against the acceptance of such a conflict. It is to be admitted from the first that the reformer had to struggle with opposition to the implementation of his ideals. Such a struggle cannot be regarded as conflict between theory and conviction but rather, at the most, between ideal and reality.

From the foregoing, the only plausible method seems to be first of all to determine the content of meaning of the "mixed form," to reveal the democratic components contained therein and, finally, to pose the question of whether and to what degree Calvin's practice corroborated his theory. It is clear that a relevant, purely historical examination can result only from a discussion of the "democratic" principles. As can be demonstrated, these served Calvin himself on certain occasions as a basis for action. In other words, one should not approach the reformer with any particular modern point of view or even a modern definition of democracy. In the final analysis, the views of "middle-class democracy" and the different socialist and communist systems differ. Therefore, a general, encompassing definition of the concept under consideration likewise may have only a highly approximate value. The result is the very real danger of attributing to the thought of the reformer ideas alien to him or concepts which have only a loose connection with the constitutional problem. . . .

If besides the mixed form described above, Calvin still considers pure aristocracy as a possible ideal, this develops from his belief, a belief borrowed from Aristotle, that the best democracies and aristocracies are not greatly different in essence and practice. Indeed, as we shall shortly see, the city-state Geneva, which Calvin had in mind as his theoretical example, exhibited, despite its democratic appearance, a heavy preponderance of aristocratic parts. The preference of the reformer for aristocracy is connected with his demand that government, if it should entirely fulfill its task, be endowed with spiritual prowess and practical intelligence. In short, the authorities must possess heroic virtues, virtues which are not merely presupposed in republican leaders but also in monarchs. If this demand coincides with the reformer's sense of reality, his recognition that the rulers of his time recklessly disturbed the balance of rights and duties, and that opposing the heightened self-confidence and the resulting arbitrary misuse of power stood only a weak sense of duty, so his vigorous stress on the virtues of the spiritually strong rulers undoubtedly developed from his voluntary-aristocratic feeling of supremacy and magnanimity, a feeling which can be designated as Christian heroism.

To be sure, this type of heroism differs basically from the heroism of the ancients and the Renaissance. Christ is also superior and magnanimous. Calvin often employs the Latin expression *animi magnitudo, magnanimitas, aequus et modestus animus, propensus animus,* which means being independent from both the oppressive and the elevating circumstances of life, independent in the sense that one permits oneself to be neither mastered by the first nor consumed in the latter. The state of his mind is a compromise between inhuman severity and tender-heartedness. But the two extremes, faint-heartedness and over-weening pride, those two extremes into which antiquity developed despite stoic magnanimity, he does not recognize. Inhuman brutality, the unshakable firmness and steadfastness which according to Cicero should characterize the magnanimous man, is not, as Calvin expressly remarks, aristocratic but rather plebeian. It is a trademark of the lowest and most blameworthy characters; it is appropriate for the lowest levels of life (*postrema ignobilitas*).

Heroic superiority has its source in the self-consciousness, in the personality of the believer. The personality should not be confused with egotism; for egotism wants to have something while the personality desires to be something. Essentially, man is clay in the hands of his Creator, but in the living relationship to God as the original source of his strength the essence and worth of man are not opposed. Rather man's essence and worth are joined in an inner unity. "This is the great thing, that we are consecrated and made holy by God, in order that we think, speak, sense, and carry out nothing but what serves His glory. The man consecrated to God may not, without doing great injustice to Him, be designated for less noble use." These words may sound too much of an aristocratic note. A possible misunderstanding will be avoided if it is made clear that all such merits are not of our own doing but rather that we owe our virtue to God. The character of the believer is not determined by his environment nor by natural laws, but by the irrevocable decree of God's Sovereignty. The categorization of the world is not the result of human reckoning and self-perceived classification; it depends not upon a human judgment derived by comparison with the way of the world, but rather it is a divine arrangement and a gift from God. The believer should be an aristocrat of the spirit in the best sense of the word because he is an aristocrat of the divine spirit, subordinated to this spirit, formed after Christ's model, endowed with purity, innocence, and simplicity. Since God cannot allow

His own to be inactive, the divine noble is obligated by divine necessity to reflect the glory of God's majesty in his entire life and to express heroically through powerful works the energy of life.

Now this characteristic described above [Christian heroism], a characteristic which Calvin had developed as a counterweight to the classical ideal personality, a characteristic which he had worked out by means of a theocentric reversal of the classical and Renaissance conception of life, applies in the strictest sense only by the religious standard, a broad standard more clearly Christian and one which denies individuality, to the elect. Nevertheless Calvin also attempted to transfer at least the most essential heroic characteristics of the Christian individual to the rulers, both Christian and non-Christian, as preconditions for their useful activity. It appears that Calvin sees in government and in its various organs circumstances of divine election, which as such are outfitted with special gifts of the Holy Spirit and serve therefore as pneumatic personalities.

The words ascribed to the reformer "that the General Council was an abuse which must be abolished," and the assertion "not the number but the importance and the meaning of the persons should decide the issue; if only quantity decided matters, then the papacy quite rightly can appeal to itself upon the greater number of its adherents," are assumed to contain a direct reference to aristocratic forms. The first quotation is based upon a slander. The latter assertion is a very arbitrary combination which does not deserve the place afforded it. In the end, one betrays an insufficient knowledge of Calvin's real motive for valuing aristocracy, if one seeks this motive in the opposition of authority and majority, an opposition conspicuously reminiscent of Stahl's formulation. For not the majority as such, not the "*popularis dominatio*" but its degenerative, the "*seditio*," Calvin condemned. What moves Calvin to prefer an aristocratic or an aristocratic-democratic form of government is, after all explanations, the conviction that the realization of the already described leadership ideal, an ideal valid for all states, can only be realized in the two indicated forms [aristocracy or mixture of aristocracy and democracy]. To the reasons already given why a monarch remains further from this ideal than a republican government, a new and important reason appears in Calvin's Commentary on Daniel. In this commentary, Calvin contends that the monarch who knows himself confronted by only the servile mass of his subjects cannot provide the necessary confidence; indeed, he must fear his subjects. For a monarch to be fearful does not suit the ruling ideal of the "*magnanimitas*"; it is prejudicial to an effective, firm government. The stability (*stabilitas*) of a state depends upon its imponderables. These can only exist in a state which possesses strict security, and where order is maintained. It is noteworthy that Calvin sets the establishment of order teleologically over that of his ruling ideal. God has stamped those who govern with the signs of His majesty, because He wants those who govern, those who are endowed with such authority, power, and intelligence, to be in a position to maintain order. The assertion of the ruling ideal with its strong characteristics and the demand that it be implemented in an appropriate, moderate, aristocratic state has as its final goal political order, a goal which comes as a necessary corollary of the organic concept. Thus, in his preference for the aristocratic state form Calvin reveals the logical working out of the central idea, the idea which lies more or less behind all his assertions, namely the organic principle.

As compared with this, the other reasons which people attribute to Calvin's favoring aristocracy are superfluous and incorrect. Some attempt to explain the reformer's preference for aristocracy from the individual psychological conditions of his personality and from the resultant aristocratic posture he held toward the necessities of social life. One finds the former in his inborn (aristocratic) inclinations which were nourished and strengthened by his relationship to a noble family and by continual contact with the upper levels of society. One finds the latter in the occasional assertions in his academic lectures, in his thoroughly unfolkish speech, and in his aristocratic outer bearing. Even if all these reasons taken together were not proven to be, on good authority, mere conjectures, Calvin's alleged disinclination toward the poor, which was also based on unsubstantiated evidence and confusion, would supply, at the most, only proof for the evaluation of his social policies, not justification for his preferring aristocracy as a political form.

John T. McNeill

CALVIN PREFERRED REPRESENTATIVE DEMOCRACY

John T. McNeill (b. 1885), Professor Emeritus of Church History at the Union Theological Seminary (New York), is dean of American historians of Calvinism. A native of Canada and an ordained Presbyterian minister, McNeill studied at McGill University, Presbyterian College (Montreal), Westminster Hall (Vancouver), the University of Edinburgh, Halle University, and the University of Chicago. He taught at several Canadian schools and the University of Chicago before going to Union Seminary in 1944 to close out his teaching career. Since his retirement in 1953, he has been a visiting professor and guest lecturer at many theological schools and universities. He is one of the general editors of the Library of Christian Classics, a contributor to many historical and religious journals, and the author of numerous books on the history of Christianity. His *History and Character of Calvinism* is the standard volume on that subject in the English language. His most recent research reflects his continuing interest in the implications of Calvin's thought for two areas of modern concern: democracy and the ecumenical movement.

AMONG the forms of government Calvin sometimes professes indifference on theoretical grounds, but on grounds of history and experience he exhibits a sharp dislike of kingship. His *Sermons on Job* (1554) contain lists of the offenses characteristic of the behavior of kings. The *Sermons on Deuteronomy* (1554–55) present sweeping denunciations of royal wickedness. In his *Lectures on Daniel* (1561) he observes the sacrilegious pride, susceptibility to flattery and other faults of King Darius, and regards these as characteristic of monarchs and accentuated in modern princes. "We today may well weep," he writes, "over the heartlessness of kings," and "over the condition of the world" in which they bear sway. "If one could uncover the hearts of kings, he would find hardly one in a hundred who does not likewise despise everything divine." In his *Sermons on Deuteronomy* (1555–56) he makes it clear that he would prefer to have rulers elected by their subjects. "When," in the days of the Judges, "God gave such a privilege to the Jews, he ratified thereby his adoption and gave proof that he had chosen them for his inheritance, and that he desired that their condition should be better and more excellent than that of their neighbors, where there were kings and princes but no liberty . . . If we have the liberty to choose judges and magistrates, since this is an excellent gift let it be pre-

From John T. McNeill, "Democratic Elements in Calvin's Thought," *Church History*, XVIII (1949), 159–164, 166–171. Reprinted by permission of *Church History* and courtesy of the author.

served and let us use it in good conscience." "If we argue about human governments we can say that to be in a free state is much better than to be under a prince." Disputes of this sort are unprofitable, but: "It is much more endurable to have rulers who are chosen and elected . . . and who acknowledge themselves subject to the laws, than to have a prince who gives utterance without reason." "Let those to whom God has given liberty and freedom (*franchise*) use it . . . as a singular benefit and a treasure that cannot be prized enough." "It is safer and more tolerable that government be in the hands of a number (*plures tenere gubernacula*), that they may be helpers of each other." Power should not be held by inheritance, and those elected should be required to render account of their service. Discussing the ancient Jewish state, he observes that the best and most desirable form of government is to have judges, that is, to be at liberty, while the laws bear sway.

Every student of Calvin's political thought must acknowledge a debt to Marc-Edouard Chenevière for his valuable monograph on that subject. But his anxiety to avoid the defects of the "liberal Protestant" interpretation of Calvin, has sometimes led him into unsafe ground. His short chapter on "Calvin and Monarchy" expresses a point of view that I for one do not find convincing, even though it is partly supported from J. Bohatec. These authors reject the position earlier adopted by G. Beyerhaus and E. Doumergue, that Calvin combatted not only the abuses, but also the principle, of monarchy. In this connection Chenevière remarks:

> If France had been ruled by a king favorable, or even simply neutral, toward the French Reformed, the sermons and commentaries of Calvin would probably have contained no complaint on the subject of monarchy. The aristocratic preferences of Calvin do not mean *ipso facto* rejection of the monarchical form of government.

In my judgment, this statement creates a somewhat misleading impression. I do not mean that Calvin ever said that no kings should exist, or that men should rid themselves of their monarchs. But his attitude to monarchy seems to me more unfavorable than Chenevière has here represented it. It is of course not accidental that his severest strictures on ancient and modern kings were uttered during the years when Mary in England and Henry II and (after 1562) Catherine de Medici in France, were putting their subjects to death by hundreds for the profession of Protestantism. Calvin also had seen such persecution on a smaller scale by Francis I, and this fact accounts for such passages as the closing paragraphs of the *Institutes*. Now, we should, I think, recognize that these facts helped to form his political ideas, and were as likely to cause a disapproval of *kingship* as to create in his mind merely a low view of *kings* in general. It is fair to say that a writer who habitually and emotionally harps on the abuses of an institution while rarely calling attention to its excellences, cannot be regarded as either a partisan of the institution or quite neutral toward it. One who persistently represents kings as abusers of their power, even though for scriptural reasons he opposes acts of rebellion against them, can hardly be regarded as indifferent to kingship itself. Let it be admitted that if kings had favored the Reformed Church, Calvin would not have scolded Darius: the fact is that they were unfavorable, and that Darius suffered for their actions in Calvin's treatment of him. This circumstance does not, I think, make it less but rather more likely that his animadversions upon Darius represent a revulsion to kingship itself, and a more or less conscious desire to create an anti-monarchical sentiment in the minds of his readers. Darius is treated as a type of kings as they are.

The statement of F. de Crue, quoted by Chenevière, that *"Calvin est un bon Français"* and that he supported the foreign policy of Henry II, must not be pressed too far. Henry's foreign policy, as it affected Germany and Switzerland, sometimes favored the Protestants of those countries. Calvin had prudential reasons for any suggestions of favor for

Henry that he expressed. Even when urging Bullinger to support an alliance of the Swiss cantons with France, he looks upon Henry as a "wicked king (May 7, 1549), and later writes to Farel, with reference to Henry and Charles V: "We should ask God to subdue their rage" (Aug. 19, 1550). Where the good cause stood to gain by the policies of kings, this was because God used them for his purposes, not from any merit of kings or kingship.

Not monarchy then, of which he is highly critical, but "aristocracy, or aristocracy tempered by democracy" is his choice. By aristocracy he means the rule of those best qualified, not of an hereditary caste. Ideally the aristocratic magistrate is one elected to his office, under that "liberty to choose judges and magistrates" which is an "excellent gift" of God. Calvin never elaborates an ample plan of representative government for the national state. He declines to sanction revolutionary efforts to overthrow monarchy, and he avoids everything of the nature of utopian incitements to change. But at heart he is a political republican. If we have the opportunity to elect our own rulers, God has favored us, and we must preserve our heritage. If God has not thus favored us, we must bear with what rulers we have.

Despite his censure of princes, Calvin has monotonously urged obedience to the ruler as a principle of the Christian life. To rebel against the ruler is to rebel against God. Assuredly it is always implied that where the honor of God is involved we must put obedience to God first. Calvin evidently implies also liberty to criticise misgovernment. This does not mean that we may resort to forcible resistance; it is frequently affirmed that the Christian under an unjust government should suffer, pray, and obey. Even an impious king may be the agent of God's judgment, and no private citizen may attack him.

For our encouragement, indeed, Calvin notes as an observation from history that God also from time to time lays tyrants low, and that He sometimes raises up powerful deliverers of the people from tyranny. In this connection his bold phrase: "Let princes hear and fear" (*audeant principes et terreantur*), sounds like a revolutionary slogan. But it is God that they are to fear. Private persons are not to assume the task of liberation. Is no resistance then permissible?

It is just here that Calvin sets ajar the iron gate of the defenses of existing absolute governments. If magistrates have been appointed for the people's protection against the license of kings (*populares magistratus ad moderandam regum libidinem constituti*), as in the case of the Spartan ephors, Roman tribunes, and Athenian demarchs, or "perhaps of the three estates" of modern kingdoms in their assemblies (*quum primarios conventus peragunt*), it would be nefarious perfidy on their part to connive at royal oppression and betray the liberty of the people, which they are under sacred obligation to defend. This single intentionally emphatic and dynamic paragraph, found in all editions of the *Institutes*, links Calvin with the more radical Calvinist political writers of the sixteenth and seventeenth centuries. Here he unbarred the gate; a phalanx of champions of the people's rights against absolute and more or less tyrannical monarchs presently entered and ultimately stormed most of the bastions. This is the second last paragraph of the Latin *Institutes*. The last enforces the rule that in questions of obedience to government we ought always to obey God rather than men. Daniel rightly disobeyed an impious royal edict, and Hosea justly condemns the obedience of Jeroboam's subjects to his demand for idolatrous worship.

Chenevière's whole interpretation tends to stress the unlikeness of Calvin's political thought to that of modern Western democracy. He holds, for example, that Calvin's *populares magistratus* while protectors of the people were in no sense their representatives, and were responsible to God alone. He minimizes Calvin's reference in this connection to the Estates General, a representative body, pointing out that the passage expresses only the possibility of an identification of the function of the Estates with that of the ancient magistrates used as examples. But, if we are looking for political principles here, let us note the nature of these examples that were, frankly and without any "perhaps," presented by Calvin in each edition of the *Institutes*. Calvin was assuredly aware that the *ephors* of Sparta, the *tribunes* of Rome and the *demarchs* of Athens were alike elected annually by popular vote and that they represented, in fact, the most democratic elements in the governmental institutions of Greece and Rome. . . .

If we test a writer's attitude to democracy by his references to "liberty, equality and fraternity," we find Calvin highly positive on the first and last of these: on equality his position is less unequivocal. . . . In his *Homilies on I Samuel* he twice refers to liberty as "an inestimable good." The Hebrew people, prizing too lightly this priceless boon, lost it when they demanded a king. Liberty is something to be held in the highest esteem and to be strenuously maintained. On the passage, "Rejoice Zebulun in thy going out and Issachar in thy tents" (Deut. 33:18), Calvin pours contempt upon Issachar as a type of those who, though strong and able, lose liberty through faintheartedness and sloth. Commenting on Deuteronomy 24:7, he speaks of liberty as "more than the half of life." There is no doubt about Calvin's espousal of liberty; but it is always a liberty limited by law and duty, and is never interpreted in revolutionary terms.

Calvin has much to say of equity, little of equality. He cannot be regarded as an egalitarian in economics or a leveller in relation to existing social and political stratifications. Yet there is emphasis on equality before the law. All are to receive equal justice, and the ruler is to have a special care for the protection of the poor and the weak. While there are different orders in society, none of these is dominant over another. There is no privileged caste depriving others of voice and rights. In the church order which Calvin instituted, laymen and clergy had equal voting status and the greatest as well as the least were subjected to the discipline. In his schools all the young had equal educational advantages regardless of birth or wealth. In December, 1557, the Little Council of Geneva instituted a plan for periodic meetings devoted to "loving and mutual censures" in which the members of this political body would "remonstrate with each other in fraternal charity." No one is more aware than Calvin that God has not made men equal in talent; but all except idiots share His gifts in nature, while all have a common need of salvation from sin. It is emphasized that humanity is a great family created of one blood.

Calvin insistently teaches a doctrine of fraternity. In his very frequent use of the words "fraternity" and "fraternal" his reference is no doubt primarily to the New Testament doctrine of divine fatherhood and brotherly love (*philadelphia*). Masters and kings are not so to domineer as to bring others into servitude. The world was not created for them: rather they were created for the multitude. Ruler and ruled have a common Creator and Father, who has endowed them with intelligence and stamped his image upon them. "He declares not only that He is Creator of the human race, of the poor as of the rich, of servants as of masters, but He calls Himself Father; thus it is needful that we have fraternity with one another; if we would not renounce the grace of our God. We see how Jesus Christ, the Lord of Glory was abased to the estate of a servant of servants . . ." The spirit of fraternity must be observed not only within the communion of the church, but in relation to society and to all men. Even the "poor pagans" knew that there could not be good government where each devoted himself to his private profit. In the state a mutual obligation exists between ruler and people, of which the law is a bond and a symbol. "The people are to be subject to their kings and the kings in turn are to obey and be subject to the laws." All the members are bound together in a mutual bond of subjection. "To embrace men in sincere love" is enjoined by natural moral law. We are to do good to all men, considering not their merit but the image of God in them. Strangers, and seemingly contemptible people bear this image: we must serve them as we serve God. "The divine image in them allures us to embrace them in the arms of our love."

We have noted the close parallel between Calvin's conceptions of church polity and of the structure of political government. In church as in state matters, he was cautious and conservative in the authorization of democratic elements. In the Reformed churches of the sixteenth century, especially those of France and Scotland, we see clearly drawn the outlines of a representative system. Calvin was not the direct author of these polities, but they were inspired in large degree by his ideas. The conservatism of his own position is shown in his attitude to a democratic project of the early years of the French Reformed Church. The Discipline adopted in 1559 provided for the admission of ministers to their office by the provincial synod, or by the colloquy (a body corresponding to the presbytery in Scottish and American Presbyterianism), not by the local consistory, nor by the congregation. A majority of the congregation, however, must approve the appointment of a minister. The Discipline also required that new members of the consistory, the local ruling body of ministers and elders, should be chosen by the consistory with the minister. Jean Morelli, a Paris minister, proposed a further democratization. He offered a plan by which the congregation would have an unrestricted right to elect its own officers. Calvin's opposition to this proposal resulted in its rejection by the national synod of Orleans in 1562, and Morelli's continued agitation finally led to his excommunication. Thus it is evident that Calvin sought to apply his idea of "aristocracy mingled with democracy" in the church no less than in the state. Against monarchy (exercised by a human agent) in the church he was of course vehemently outspoken. This condemnation applies not only to the papacy but to the hierarchical order. It is wrong that men are made bishops "by permission of the pope" and by action of the canons in such manner that "the people's right to choose has been wholly taken away." Calvin restored this right, with cautious restrictions, in Geneva and approved everywhere a reference of certain important matters, including the settlement of pastors, to the vote of the people. With this element of democracy, the system he approved contained the element of aristocracy, in the ordination of pastors and elders who formed essentially self-perpetuating bodies within the Christian community.

"Democracy" is not a term in favor with Calvin. He does not advocate democracy in and of itself: he fears its deterioration into anarchy. Nevertheless, his notion of "aristocracy tempered by democracy" approaches our conception of representative democracy. It becomes unmistakably clear in his later writings that the ideal basis of government is election by the citizens.

Perhaps it was because he shrank from every suggestion of revolution that Calvin presented nothing of the nature of a blue-print for a system of representative government for the national state. He utterly distrusts government directly by the masses. The middle way of an elective "aristocracy" is his solution. Consistent with this was his policy in Geneva. He found Geneva an autonomous city whose armed citizens had shaken off feudal and episcopal control. It was in a stage of post-revolution instability. A government by elective councils and by the general meeting of citizens was taking shape. The changes effected in Calvin's time, for which he was largely, though in uncertain degree, responsible, centered control more closely in the Little Council and the four Syndics. Proposals for legislation had to pass in turn the Little Council, the Council of Sixty, the Council of Two Hundred, and the Grand Council of all citizens. The Council of Two Hundred was composed of nominees of the Little Council, and the majority of the members of the Little Council were chosen by the Two Hundred. This interlocking of the councils was an oligarchical element, but correctives of oligarchy are also in evidence. The meeting of citizens once a year elected the four Syndics who were the chief administrators and judges of the city; and it chose to this office, by secret ballot, two from the wealthier and two from the poorer class of citizens. It also elected the commander of the militia, and some other officials. In February, 1560, Calvin addressed the General Assembly of citizens urging them "to choose (their magistrates) with a pure conscience, without regard to anything but the honor and glory of God, for the safety and defense of the republic." Thus the chief rulers were not an established aristocracy either of birth or of special privilege. The elective principle was retained in this conservative democracy—for we may so designate the system; and since the principal elections were annual, there was a considerable shift of public servants.

Calvin never took to himself any political office or title and, although ridicule of him and of the other ministers was made a punishable offense, he never used soldiers to protect his person. As Pierre Mesnard points out, "he was not king, mayor, president or protector." He was not eligible for political office, since he was not a citizen, until the end of the year 1559. Until 1555 his position was quite insecure: although thereafter it was not in fact endangered, at any time a popular movement could have thrown him out by constitutional means. Within the church he was permitted to erect a system of discipline that was rigorous and intolerant. Calvin was masterful, sometimes vindictive, and often harsh; but politically he used constitutional methods and won his way (when he got it) by the persuasion of his fervid oratory. Under his leadership Geneva became a firmly established republic; quite conceivably, if more had been left to the council of citizens, factions would have destroyed the stability of the government.

In a single sentence Calvin defines what he thinks the ideal government: "I readily acknowledge that no kind of government is more happy than this, where liberty is regulated with becoming moderation, and properly established on a durable basis (*ad diuturnitatem*)." No doubt he felt that Geneva was attaining to this status of regulated and enduring liberty, though we today would be far from content with the "liberty" that remained under the "regulation."

Herbert Darling Foster

CALVIN AND HIS FOLLOWERS CHAMPIONED REPRESENTATIVE GOVERNMENT

Herbert Darling Foster (1863–1927) was for years one of America's most distinguished and articulate advocates of the thesis that Calvinism is one of the major sources of modern democracy. Himself a child of the manse, Foster possessed an intimate knowledge of both the spirit and history of Calvinism. He earned an A.B. at Dartmouth College in 1885 and an A.M. at Harvard in 1892. He did further graduate work and research at the Universities of Cambridge, Berlin, Paris, London and Geneva, receiving an Litt.D. degree from the last-named institution in 1909. He taught at Worcester College from 1885 until he became professor of history at Dartmouth in 1893, where he remained until his death. His major contributions to historical research, including his work on the history of Calvinism, are included in *The Collected Papers of Herbert Darling Foster,* published in his memory in 1929.

"IN our account of these sons of Geneva, we will begin with the father of the faithful; faithful, I mean, to their old antimonarchical doctrines and assertions; and that is, the great mufti of Geneva, who in the fourth book of his Institutions, chapter 20, section 31, has the face to own such doctrine to the world as this." In such wise, a royalist sermon of 1663 introduced the famous section from Calvin's *Institutes* containing the germ of the Calvinistic theory of constitutional resistance to tyranny through the people's representatives. In the Elizabethan English of Norton's translation, familiar to English, Scottish, and American readers from the Reformation to the American Revolution, Calvin's pregnant sentences ran thus:

> Though the correcting of unbridled government be the revengement of the Lord, let us not by and by think that it is committed to us, to whome there is given no other commaundment but to obey and suffer. I speake alway of private men. For if there be at this time any magistrates for the behalfe of the people, (such as in olde time were the Ephori, that were set against the Kinges of Lacedemonia, or the Tribunes of the people, against the Romane Consuls: or the Demarchy, against the Senate of Athenes: and the same power also which peradventure as things are nowe the three estates have in everie realme when they hold their principall assemblies) I doe so not forbid them according to their office to withstande the outraging licentiousness of kinges: that I affirme that if they winke at kinges wilfully raging over and treading downe the poor communaltie, their dissembling is not without wicked breache of faith, because they deceitfully betray the libertie of the people, whereof they know themselves to bee appointed protectors by the ordinance of God.

Calvin's *Institutes,* containing this theory of constitutional resistance through representative magistrates, remained for centuries a standard book among Protestants. Probably no other theological work was so widely read and so influential from the Reformation to the American Revolution. At least seventy-four editions in nine languages, besides fourteen abridgments, appeared before the Puritan exodus to America, an

From Herbert Darling Foster, "The Political Theories of Calvinists Before the Puritan Exodus to America," *American Historical Review,* XXI (1916), 481–487, 489–494, 496–503. Reprinted by permission of the American Historical Association.

average of one edition annually for three generations. Huguenots, Scots, Dutchmen, Walloons, Palatines, and other Germans, and an overwhelming majority of the American colonists of the seventeenth century were bred on its strong political theories as well as on the strong meat of its theology. In England the *Institutes* was considered "the best and perfectest system of divinity" by both Anglican and Puritan, until Laud's supremacy. In 1578 (with Calvin's Catechism) it was required of Oxford undergraduates. Curious witness to its grip upon men was borne by Laud in 1636. Admitting that the *Institutes* "may profitably be read as one of the first books of divinity," Laud secretly endeavored to dissuade New College students from reading it "so soon." "I am afraid it . . . doth too much possess their judgments . . . and makes many of them humorous in, if not against the church."

In Scotland the passage quoted from Calvin's *Institutes* was cited in defense of Mary's deposition, by Knox and the commissioners to Elizabeth. In England not only Cartwright and the other authors of the *Admonition to Parliament* but also their opponent Whitgift and even the Anglican Elborow as late as 1636 utilized the authority of the *Institutes*. Quoted by widely read New England Puritans, like Governor Bradford, Cotton, Hooker, Roger Williams, Jonathan Edwards, and by Puritan preachers before Parliament during the Civil War, and controverted by Royalists later in the century, it continued to be spread in the eighteenth century through numerous citations in the popular Bayly's *Practice of Piety*, which went through fifty-nine editions in seven languages by 1759. Men of a somewhat different sort were probably influenced, directly or indirectly, through the citations by a remarkable list of men widely read and quoted in Europe and America —"the judicious Hooker," Milton, Harrington, Sidney, Locke, and Rousseau. The demand for the *Institutes* in English translation is suggested by the nine editions before the Civil War (and apparently about ten between 1763 and and 1863, six of these being American editions); and further by its appearance in the London *Catalogue of Approved Divinity Books*, 1655, 1657, and the *Catalogue of Most Vendible Books in England*, 1657, 1658.

Of some work of Calvin at least 435 editions appeared before the founding of New England, an average of one every ten weeks. Most colonial libraries seem to contain some work by Calvin and scarcely a colonial list of books from New Hampshire to South Carolina appears to lack books written by Calvinists.

Calvin's teaching of constitutional resistance to tyranny logically followed his fundamental premises of the absolute sovereignty of God and the "Word of God"; for that absolute authority limited all "earthly princes" and made both king and representative magistrate "responsible to God and men." Calvin moreover pictured that "singular and truly sovereign power of God" not as "idly beholding from Heaven," "but as holding the helm of the universe."

Calvin's teaching of the "breach of faith" by the representative magistrates, if they "betray the liberties of the people, whereof they knowe themselves to bee appointed protectors by the ordinaunce of God," was within a year followed by the enforcement in Geneva of another fundamental tenet of Calvinists—a covenant. The Genevan Confession of 1537, submitted by Calvin and Farel, was a religious rather than a political covenant. But a civil ordinance commanded under pain of exile "all burghers, inhabitants and subjects to swear to guard and observe" this creed-covenant, which included the ten commandments, and emphasized morals more than theology. This creed-covenant was moreover defended by Calvin on the basis of the covenants made by the Israelites under Moses, Josiah, Asa, and "the admirable defenders of liberty, Ezra and Nehemiah," examples constantly cited by Calvinists in their political covenants for a century to come.

After seven years' experience in Switzerland and Germany Calvin advocated as the best form of government "either aristocracy of a mixture of aristocracy and democracy" such as "the

Lord established among the people of Israel." Sixteen more years' observation of the "imperfections of men" led the ripened statesman to advocate constitutional government (*politia*) "in the hands of many . . . so that if any one arrogate to himself more than is right, the many may act as censors and masters to restrain his ambition." This "mixture of aristocracy and democracy" was the form of government in most Calvinistic industrial communities and self-governing commonwealths. Such representative government was regularly exemplified in their churches and logically advocated for the state. A striking example illustrates this chain of religious-political Calvinistic influence. Thomas Cartwright during his exile taught theology in Geneva and before leaving obtained permission to attend the consistory in order to report to England upon the Genevan representative church government. Immediately on his return to England he advocated in his *Admonition to Parliament* a like system of representative government in the Church, and then maintained that the State should follow the Church's model. Cartwright's reasoning, often quoted approvingly by Hooker of Connecticut to Cotton of Massachusetts, was requoted by Cotton to Say and Sele in England.

Calvin himself, toward the end of his career, advocated in theory and practice representative government "by common consent" in both Church and State as the "best condition by far"; "and even when men become kings by hereditary right this does not seem consistent with liberty."

Before his death Calvin had combined the theory of constitutional resistance through divinely ordained representatives with two other Calvinistic theories, that of a compact and that of a fundamental written law.

> Inasmuch as kings and princes pledge their faith to the people by an oath, it is fair to ask, if they break faith, whether the people may not themselves consult together and apply a fit remedy. The question is certainly difficult and it would not be convenient or expedient to discuss it now; for we see many seeking opportunity for innovations and allowing too great changes. Subjects themselves may not rebel against even tyrannical rulers. . . . Nevertheless, certain remedies against tyranny are allowable, for example when magistrates and estates have been constituted, to whom has been committed the care of the commonwealth: they shall have power to keep the prince to his duty and even to coerce him if he attempt anything unlawful.

Samuel's "reading to the people and recording in a book" "the law of the kingdom," in order to show "the mutual obligation of head and members," Calvin recommends as an example; "for every commonwealth rests upon laws and agreements . . . by which as by a bridle each is held to his calling." He advocates written statutes that "recourse may be had to the written law." The *lex scripta* he describes as "nothing but an attestation of the *lex naturae*, whereby God brings back to memory what has already been imprinted on our hearts."

From Calvin's premises of the supreme authority of God and his Word, we find him then developing these permanent contributions to political theory and practice. The absolute supremacy of God and of his Word ("obey God rather than man") demands not passive but active resistance. This resistance is not the privilege of private individuals but the obligation of divinely ordained representatives "responsible to God and the people," such as councillors, estates, or parliaments. Such resistance is constitutional, rational, and orderly because based on and tested by three things greatly emphasized by Calvin and his disciples: (1) a written religious document, "the open Word of God," to be interpreted with "equity and reason"; (2) a political covenant or compact, preferably written, for example a coronation oath; (3) some form of fundamental law, *lex naturae, principes d'équité*, or *quelque semence de droicture*.

Calvin's followers, usually accustomed to some form of representative government—local or national—and to written charters, and trained still further by their representative system of church discipline and government, exhibited the Calvinistic spirit of "going forward [*cheminer*] each according to his station and employing faithfully for the maintenance of the republic whatever God has given them." They therefore developed his theories, further combined them on the basis of growing experience, incorporated them into public law, and proved them practicable. In the Biblical commonwealth of Geneva, citizen and refugee were profoundly convinced of the righteousness of the Calvinistic theories. When a domineering military officer, opponent of Calvin's policy, attempted to wrest from a Genevan syndic his staff of office, the magistrate replied: "This staff has been given me not by you but by God and the people, to whom I shall return it and not to you." The little republic of Geneva, bred upon Calvin's *Institutes*, catechism, and consistory, itself was a striking and influential exemplification of the successful embodiment of Calvin's political theories into what we may venture to call the first Puritan state. "Let not Geneva be forgotten or despised. Religious liberty owes it much respect, Servetus notwithstanding," wrote the second President of the United States. . . .

In 1558 three pastors and one elder of "the Englishe Churche and Congregation at Geneva" (three at least being translators of the Genevan version of the Bible) printed there eight political addresses to England and Scotland. Christopher Goodman's *How Superior Powers ought to be obeyed and wherein they may lawfully by God's Worde be disobeyed and resisted* (which Calvin pronounced "somewhat harsh" and to "be handled with caution," yet "admitted to be true") advocates resistance on the basis of the supremacy of God's laws, responsibility of representatives, and a mutual covenant. "You promised obedience to your Superiors, that they might helpe you," "to defend God's Lawes." "If they will do so, and keep promise with you accordinge to their office, then do you owe unto them all humble obedience: If not, you are discharged, and no obedience belongeth to them: because they are not obedient to God." This passage Milton quotes in his *Tenure of Kings*. Goodman, like Ponet and Melville, asserts that the people were not "created of God to serve their kinges," but "their kinges appoynted of God to preserve his people, whereof they are but a portion and a member." Like Ponet, Goodman takes a step beyond Calvin in maintaining that "it apperteyeth not onely to the Magistrates and al other inferior officers to see that their Princes be subject to Gods Lawes, but to the common people also."

John Knox's letter of 1558 "To the Commonalty of Scotland" likewise desired not only the "Estates and Nobilitie" but also "the Communaltie, my Brethren," to "compell your Byshoppes and Clergie to cease their tyrannie and answer by the scriptures of God." From Calvinistic premises, including Asa's covenant, Knox draws two Calvinistic conclusions: "the first, That no idolatour can be exempted from punishment by Goddes Law. The seconde is, That the punishment of such crimes, as are idolatries, blasphemie, and others, that tuche the Majestie of God, dothe not appertaine to kinges and chefe rulers only, but also the whole bodie of that people, and to every membre of the same, *according to the vocation of everie man, and according to that possibilitie and occasion which God doth minister to revenge the injury done his glorie.*" "Moste justely may the same men depose and punishe him that unadvysedly before they did electe." . . .

Evidence of Calvinistic and Genevan influence upon Scotland is found in the *Acts of Parliament and Assembly*, the Confession of Faith, the Genevan order of worship, and the "Buke of Discipline" 's system of church government by representative laymen. It is also testified to directly. The assembly desired the judgment of Calvin upon resistance to rulers. Knox affirmed that he had "heard the judgementis" and "come nocht to this Realme without." "A written defence of the Scotch presented to Queen Elizabeth," quoted by von Raumer, mentions the approval of Calvin and Melanchthon.

Through the marginal notes of four Calvinistic versions of the Bible, teachings of covenant obligation to constitutional resistance passed into the political thought of two continents. The Genevan version, "the common Bible of the people and even of scholars" for three-quarters of a century, went through over one hundred editions before 1617. On this "Breeches Bible" were bred Shakespeare and the founders of the American colonies and the English Commonwealth. Scores of marginal notes on covenant, vocation, rights of the "congregation," deposition of kings, the supremacy of God's Word, and the duty of orderly resistance to tyranny, appear in the Genevan version, Junius and Tremellius's *Biblia Sacra,* Beza's Latin text of the New Testament (in its eighty-eight editions before 1640, common property in Continental, English, and colonial libraries), and in the *Annotations* by the Westminster Assembly of Divines. Such widespread sanction for Calvinistic political theories through the Bibles in the homes of scholar and common man enormously enhanced the appeal of Calvinistic writers and preachers in France, Holland, the Palatinate, Scotland, England, and America.

The Calvinistic theory and practice of constitutional resistance to tyranny, especially as exemplified in Scotland, was formulated in the *History of Scotland,* and in the *De Jure Regni apud Scotos* (1579) by Buchanan, a Calvinistic scholar in politics, who was moderator of the General Assembly which demanded Mary's "demission" and a "mutual and reciprocal contract" between prince and people, and who also aided in the indictment of Mary before Elizabeth. . . .

The Huguenot churches, organized in 1559, rapidly developed a local and national representative system through local consistory, district colloquy, provincial assembly, and national synod. The synods especially developed marvellous efficiency, and eventually assumed nearly all the distinctive functions of a state—financial, military, administrative, legislative—and were sometimes called "États Généraux." In 1594 the Huguenots closely followed their ecclesiastical model in the organization of their political national assembly based upon provincial assemblies and colloquies.

> They have begun to spread among the populace the idea that the King has his authority from the people, and that the subject is not obliged to obey the Prince when he commands anything which is not to be found in the New Testament. And they are on the highroad to reduce that province to the condition of a democratic state like Switzerland,

wrote the Venetian Suriano.

In 1573 two Huguenot exiles in Geneva, Hotman and Beza, talked over the situation after St. Bartholomew, and produced two books advocating more radical theories than Calvin's. The *Franco-Gallia* of Hotman, for eleven years teacher or professor of law in Geneva, "distinctly proves" (asserted Sidney), on historical and legal grounds, that in France "the people (that is the assembly of the estates) had entire power both of electing and deposing their kings." . . .

The *Franco-Gallia* follows Calvin's *Institutes* in picturing the "easy lapse" from royalty to tyranny and the necessity of constitutional restraint through representatives of the people. Reference to Calvin was dangerous in France, therefore Plato is given as author of the sentiment. Plato however taught that tyranny springs from democracy. Finally, to his other Calvinistic remedies against tyranny, the Huguenot lawyer adds the supreme visible authority of "la parole de Dieu."

The *Franco-Gallio* was widely read and Hotman's influence is directly traceable among Huguenots, Puritans, and liberals.

Beza's *Droit des Magistrats,* shown to Hotman and written simultaneously with the *Franco-Gallia* in 1573, thus develops Calvinistic premises and conclusions.

"There is not other will but God's alone which is perpetual and immutable, the principle of all justice." Princes are to be obeyed if they do not violate "the first table of the law of God," or "what one owes to his neighbor according to his vocation public or private." "Peoples . . . are more ancient than their magistrates, and consequently the people are not created for their magistrates, but on the contrary the magistrates for the people; as the tutor for the pupil." Tyrants "are not legitimate kings," and therefore "should be opposed by all." Beza cannot "condemn all tyrannicides without exception." Though private individuals should seek remedy "through their lawful magistrates," "if the magistrate fails to do his duty, then each private individual should with all his power maintain the lawful status of his country, to which, after God, everyone owes his allegiance, against him who is not his magistrate since he wishes to usurp or has usurped domination in violation of law."

Though he here goes beyond Calvin, Beza's characteristic appeal is to the responsible authorities. He urges the duty of everyone to co-operate in securing "the common lawful assembly" and the enforcement ("by those whose function it is, *when God gives them power*") of "the compacts and edicts already lawfully granted." Beza here advocates precisely what the Huguenots to his knowledge (not improbably with his advice) had been attempting through both civil and church officers, namely, functional responsibility, and insistence on rights guaranteed to Huguenots by royal edicts.

"There exists a *mutuelle obligation* between king and magistrate": each is bound by oath to see that the other does not violate "certain conditions." If the king "manifestly violates the conditions on which he has been accepted," the magistrates are "freed from their oath, at least so far as to be justified in opposing the manifest oppression of the kingdom they have sworn to defend, according to their calling and particular function." "The nations, so far as justice and equity have prevailed, have neither created nor accepted their kings save on certain conditions; if these are manifestly violated, it follows that those who had the power to grant kings such authority have no less power to deprive them of it." This power lies especially with the "Estates or others ordained to serve as bridle to sovereigns"; "and those whose duty it is can and should take it in hand, if they do not wish to violate the oath they have taken to God and their country."

Beza significantly joins together "God and the Estates" as charged with the deposing of kings; maintains that "the Estates are above kings"; and denies that subjects "break faith when each within the limits of his vocation hinders the course of tyranny." He appeals to *droit de nature, generale et universelle equite*, and *droit de gens* as fundamental law. Proceeding then from the sovereignty of God and the law of God, Beza, Calvin's colleague and successor, develops these theories: (1) the sovereignty of the people represented by their estates and elective magistrates; (2) the responsibility of these representatives to God and the people; (3) the mutual compact of king and representatives; (4) the subjection of both to fundamental law; (5) the consequent obligation of constitutional resistance to tyranny.

The influence of Beza was enormous. His writings were quoted or his counsel directly asked by Huguenots, Dutch, Germans, Scots, English Puritans, and American colonists. The bitter criticisms of him and his "Genevian ideas" witness his authority. Whitgift complained to Beza of his attempts in England and Scotland, through seven different publications, to "obtrude the Geneva discipline upon all churches and . . . bring back . . . a Democracy." On an average, one edition of his Latin Testament, teaching political Calvinism through its annotations, appeared annually, and some one of his works in English dress semi-annually, for a half-century. A fresh edition of Beza and Marot's Psalms, made more inspiring by their militant music, appeared every three weeks for four years.

Le Politique, Dialogue . . . de l'Authorité des Princes et de la Liberté des Peuples illustrates the familiar Calvinistic theories in many anonymous Huguenot pamphlets appearing after St. Bartholomew. "Every power is of God"; the "people's deputies," or "ephors," "established by God and nature" (who have received the oath of kings to obey the laws, and who have made and may unmake kings), are in duty bound to fulfill their function and prevent tyranny if the king violates his oath, the laws he has covenanted to keep, the edicts he has granted, or the "sovereign law of God and nature." . . .

In the Netherlands, revolt was justified upon Calvinistic theories by William the Silent and his Genevan-bred advisers. William maintained that he was "one of the chief members of the Estates," and "the Estates have been instituted to put a check upon the tyranny of the prince." "The king is only inaugurated after having sworn to observe the law." "He violated the law . . . the prince of Orange is therefore freed of his oaths." "Lawfully called as the vindicator of liberty and the savior of an oppressed people by a divine and human call, he is bound thereto by the function which he exercises. Let all therefore who do not oppose themselves to the will of God comprehend that each according to the measure of his duty in virtue of the obedience due to God, country, laws, and magistrates must second the efforts of the Prince of Orange."

Marnix St. Aldegonde, the Genevan-bred theologian and diplomat, and right-hand man of William, answered his request for advice thus: "Men have taken arms by the advice and authority of the Estates General of the country, which have a lawful vocation from God against an oppressor of the country and a sworn and irreconcilable enemy of all servants of God." "If they reject a prince who is offered them for their defense against tyranny, they are ungrateful toward God, rebellious against His will and merit coming under the yoke."

Nine months after the receipt of this reply William, in his justification of the revolt addressed to the Estates General, strikingly illustrated the Calvinistic teachings of covenant, ephors, and representative responsibility. The ruler "by his oath purposes that in case of contravention we should not be longer bound to him." "Between all lords and vassals there is a mutual obligation. . . . Among other rights we have this privilege of serving our dukes as the ephors served their kings in Sparta, that is, to keep the royalty firm in the hand of a good prince and to bring to reason him who contravenes his oath." "The assembly of the estates, a bridle and bar to tyranny, hated by tyrants, and loved by true princes, is the sole foundation of a state." Failure to constrain the ruler is perjury.

Seven months later the Estates General of the Netherlands, like the Parliament of Scotland, put Calvinistic theory into practice, embodying its teaching of constitutional resistance in a document having the force of public law in the Netherlands, the Dutch Declaration of Independence, 1581. "A prince is constituted by God to be ruler of a people, to defend them from oppression." "God did not create the people slaves to their prince, to obey commands, whether right or wrong, but rather the prince for the sake of the subjects." "And when he . . . on the contrary, oppresses them, seeking opportunities to infringe their ancient customs and privileges . . . then he is no longer a prince, but a tyrant." "When this is done deliberately, unauthorized by the states, they may not only disallow his authority, but legally proceed to the choice of another prince for their defence. . . . This is what the law of nature dictates for the defense of liberty . . . more justifiable in our land . . . for most of the Provinces receive their prince upon certain conditions, which he swears to maintain; which, if the prince violates, he is no longer sovereign." . . .

The Estates of the Netherlands therefore, in accordance with their natural and civil rights, deposed the King of Spain rightly, for nothing is more natural or lawful than the annulling of a contract which one of the two parties has broken. . . .

In Germany, five representative Calvinists, three of whom had come into personal relations with Geneva, maintained the obligation of the representative magistrate to resist the tyrant. Zanchius, exile from Italy, and professor at Strassburg and Heidelberg, maintained, on the basis of the frequently quoted Scriptural and classical passages and examples, that "resistance to the superior magistrate commanding evil is not resistance to a power ordained by God." "We ought to obey God rather than man." "If for the sake of religion you oppose yourself to the King, you oppose yourself not to power but to tyranny, and unless you so oppose yourself you act contrary to divine and human law."

Zanchius had lived in Geneva, worked vigorously for the introduction of Calvinistic church discipline into the Palatinate, served as an elder at Heidelberg, and was asked by Calvin to come to Geneva. His books were widely owned and read.

Another cosmopolitan, the Italian exile, Peter Martyr, twice invited to Geneva by Calvin, spread the latter's political theories through twenty years' residence in Strassburg, Oxford, and Zürich, and through his widely read *Loci Communes* and commentaries. Martyr taught that the private man may not revolt; but that "the lesser powers" like the "ephors and Roman tribunes" or "Imperial Electors" who "elect the superior powers and govern the Republic with fixed laws," may use force to compel a prince "to fulfill conditions and compacts (*pacta*) to which he has taken oath." Unlike Melanchthon and like a true Calvinist, he teaches active and not passive resistance.

The famous German publicist, Althusius, professor of law at Herborn, and a courageous magistrate at Emden for thirty-six years, maintained in his *Politica Methodice Digesta* (1603) the Calvinistic teaching of the duties of the ephors and estates ordained by God. Althusius had apparently lived at Geneva; he certainly acknowledged his indebtedness to Gothofredus, a Genevan professor of law; exercised the function of a Calvinistic elder in the church at Emden; and "in all his works betrays a strong Calvinistic spirit." He taught that if the sovereign breaks the contract between him and the people he loses his divine authority and the people exercise the divine will in deposing him. Gierke notes in Althusius, in common with other Calvinists, these characteristic traits of political thought: use of the Scripture for determining the outward form of Church and State; predominance of Old Testament examples; emphasis of the decalogue in politics; admiration for Jewish law and form of state; rejection of canon law; presbyterian and synodal church organization; and cooperation of Church and State. "Finally, in the formation of the constitution of the state in all of these Calvinistic political writers, there are certain common positive traits which hark back to the propositions of Calvin, and particularly to his teaching of the ephors and their rights and duties to act against unrighteous rulers." Gierke then cites the famous section from the last chapter of Calvin's *Institutes* quoted at the beginning of this article.

This conception of a power conferred indirectly by God and directly by the people was expressed ten years later by a Heidelberg professor, " Pareus, a German divine, but fully cast into the Genevan mould."

"The proper and first cause of the magistrate is God himself; but men are the proximate causes." "Subjects not private citizens, but appointed as inferior magistrates, may justly, even by arms, defend the commonwealth and church or religion against a superior magistrate," under certain conditions, "because even the higher magistrate is subject to divine laws and his commonwealth." "The law of God not only prohibits tyranny, but also commands that it be legitimately checked." Pareus's teaching of the right of deposition of kings is thus translated by Milton in his *Tenure of Kings:* "They whose part is to set up magistrates, may restrain them also from outrageous deeds, or pull them down; but all magistrates are set up either by parliament or by electors, or by other magistrates; they therefore, who exalted them may lawfully degrade and punish them." . . .

A fourth German widely read, Alstedius of Nassau, member of the Synod of Dort, maintained the characteristic theories of Calvinists: the subjection of all to the *lex naturae* and to the Bible; obedience to laws rather than to kings; the right of the entire body of subjects to resist tyrants upon violation of oath; the function of "ephors" or estates of the realm to appoint, judge, and depose the king and exercise *summa auctoritas* especially in extraordinary taxes.

Resistance to tyrants did not originate with Calvinists, nor did the idea remain peculiar to them. It had been proclaimed by scriptural, classical, and medieval writers; it was advocated by Lutheran and Catholic. The Calvinist provided a method of resistance that was at once definite, legal, and practicable; combined it with other theories and sound experiences of self-governing churches and civil communities; and finally worked it out into something of world significance—responsible, representative, constitutional government. Where Aquinas taught passive resistance, Zanchius, quoting Aquinas, "took the next step" and urged active resistance. In case of "irreligious and iniquitous commands," said Beza, "it is not enough not to do evil, but we must acquit ourselves of that which we owe God and our neighbor." Lutherans who proclaimed and practiced active resistance at Magdeburg met criticism at Wittenberg; they found sympathy at Geneva, where Calvin sided with them against Melanchthon, and Beza ascribed his anonymous revolutionary treatise to "those of Magdeburg."

That the Jesuits and the Catholic "Monarchomachi" of the sixteenth century took a leaf from the Calvinistic book of political theory is itself a witness to the ever-widening political influence of Calvinists. These Catholic writers however retained the canon law; minimized the dignity and power of the State; and in neither Church nor State developed government and discipline by representative bodies of laymen, as did the Calvinists. The Calvinist rejected the canon law; insisted that civil magistrates were "ordained by the divine law of God" and were "not a human ordinance"; laid less emphasis upon tyrannicide and more upon representative government and nationality. More significant still, he definitely established constitutional government. His ideas of "vocation," representative responsibility, compact, and fundamental written law were embodied in a series of documents which formed the working basis of successful constitutional governments in a series of Puritan states—usually with a significant federal element—Geneva, the United Netherlands, the English Commonwealth, Scotland under the Solemn League and Covenant, the New England Confederation and its constituent Puritan commonwealths, and, in practice if not in legal theory, certain New England self-governing communities. . . .

The Church through its lay government and severe discipline showed magistrate and common man what it was to exercise representative responsibility in making and enforcing law regardless of rank, and in accordance with a written fundamental law, "the open Word of God," and some form of written church constitution. Then Beza, the Huguenot *États Généraux*, Scottish Covenanters, William of Orange, Cartwright, Hooker, Cotton, and Winthrop logically advocated a similar form of government in the State, and wherever possible established it.

Their sound principles of six days' labor weekly of every man at his "calling," the right to take interest, the obligation to produce, "lay something by," and give away, enabled Calvinists to found economically self-sufficient states, successful enough to attract desirable population, productive and progressive enough to maintain liberal expenditures for education, religion, social betterment, and constitutional government.

Their political theories could never have found such effective utterance and fulfilment had there not been behind all theory the dynamics of Calvinism—the trained conscience, brain, and will of sturdy, clear-minded, businesslike men of affairs, rulers of cities and founders of states, devoted each to his "vocation" to which every man had been called by the ceaseless will of "The Eternal" who "held the helm of the universe." "They had to the highest degree the force that made them strong: character. They knew whither they were going, what they wished and what they could do." They possessed what for lack of a simpler term might be called the co-operative social energy of clear-eyed individualists. The dynamics of Calvinism are revealed in Calvin's "unterrified we shall go on in our calling" . . . "ad ultimum usque spiritum"; in the pride in being "ane watchman" and "a profitable member within the Commonwealth" of Knox, "who never feared the face of man"; in Andrew Melville's "we dar and will"; Beza's exhortation to "succor our brethren according to our power and vocation"; Mornay's dictum, "it is stupid to feel in one's self the power to do something well and not seek out the means of doing it"; and Aldegonde's motto "repos d'ailleurs."

With real political insight, the Calvinist grasped the possibilities involved in the combination of the theories of: (1) "vocation," (2) representative "responsibility to God and the people," (3) fundamental and written law of God and man, to which (4) king, representatives, and people were bound by mutual compact. With characteristic temper he "went forward," not resting until he had demonstrated the practicability of these ideas and established both constitutional resistance and constitutional government. Once embodied in edict, statute, or charter, in Geneva, France, Holland, Scotland, England, and America, these theories were appealed to with relentless Calvinistic logic as public and fundamental law. The additional facts that such laws "aggrie with the law of God" and that they were rewarded with the prosperity promised by God were logically pointed out, by believers in universal providence and the reign of law, as evidence of the soundness of their principles and as "public proof of the Agency of God." The Calvinist based his political theories upon his faith in an almighty providence and found his actual institutions confirming his faith.

Robert M. Kingdon

CALVIN'S FOLLOWERS FEARED DEMOCRACY

Robert M. Kingdon (b. 1927) has been Professor of History at the University of Wisconsin since 1965. His undergraduate degree is from Oberlin College and his doctorate from Columbia University. He has edited and written several books and articles on sixteenth-century history including *Geneva and the Coming of the Wars of Religion,* published in 1956. The following is a selection from an article which served as the preliminary sketch for his most recent book, *Geneva and the Consolidation of the French Protestant Movement.*

THE idea that Calvinism provided an important source of political democracy was long a popular one in this country. Careful studies of Calvin's own political ideas exploded a part of that theory several decades ago. There remained in some quarters the belief that the Calvinist introduction into church government of some popular participation helps to explain the rise of democratic civil government. Recent studies have cast doubt even on this argument from analogy. There were periods in the early history of the Calvinist move-

From Robert M. Kingdon, "Calvinism and Democracy: Some Political Implications of Debates on French Reformed Church Government, 1562–1572," *American Historical Review,* LXIX (1964), 393–394, 395–401. Reprinted by permission of the author.

ment, however, when the argument from analogy was taken seriously. They deserve further study. One such period was the decade 1562–1572, beginning shortly before Calvin's death in 1564, extending until the St. Bartholomew's massacres in 1572.

During this decade, the Reformed church that Calvin had founded in France was rocked by a bitter running quarrel that assumed significant proportions. One faction within that church argued that Christian church government should be highly decentralized, with local congregations assuming virtual autonomy and with laymen playing a significant role in their leadership. In short, they wanted what we might call congregationalism. Another faction insisted on strengthening the centralizing institutions in Reformed church government, particularly the provincial and national synods, and the peculiarly powerful Geneva mother church, with ordained clergymen assuming real leadership at every level. What they wanted is what we would call presbyterianism. Both sides argued vigorously for their views with that blend of arguments drawn from scriptural exegesis, early church history, and prudential political considerations, which was typical of their time and milieu.

The chief protagonists in this debate were Jean Morely, sire de Villiers, and Theodore Beza. Morely was the founder of the "congregational" faction. He was a French Reformed petty nobleman, whose writings reveal him to have been a man of modest education, and whose most important position was as tutor for several months at the court of Navarre, to the young prince who was eventually to become King Henry IV of France. Beza was chief defender of the "presbyterian" position. He was also of a French petty noble family, but was a brilliant product of the best that the French Renaissance educational system could offer and had become Calvin's undisputed successor as ecclesiastical leader of the French-speaking Reformed churches. He served for decades as Moderator of the Geneva Company of Pastors. He influenced key decisions by a number of important French national synods and even presided over the most important of them. And he was the chief ecclesiastical adviser to the great aristocrats who provided political and military leadership to the party. . . .

Of the many ideas about ecclesiastical polity and discipline debated by these two factions during this decade, one is of particular interest to the historian of political thought. This is the idea that there is analogy between civil government and ecclesiastical government. Not all who were parties to the dispute would even concede the validity of this great analogy. Those who did drew diametrically different conclusions from it. But for those who were willing to pursue the notion of analogy, the concept of democracy became an inevitable part of the debate. The sharpest and most interesting demonstrations of this fact are to be found in the writings of the two chief protagonists, Morely and Beza. Specifically, they are found in certain passages of a book titled *Traicté de la discipline & police chrestienne,* which Morely had published in 1562 and which remained the essential statement of his faction's position even though it was apparently never reprinted, and in certain passages of letters written by Beza in 1571 and thereafter to counter the influence of Ramus, at a time when the length of the controversy and the prospect of complete victory led him to be somewhat more blunt than he had been earlier.

Morely's book was prepared with the idea of an analogy between civil government and ecclesiastical government central to his plan of writing and was to be the first volume in a set of two. It dealt with the form of ecclesiastical government that Morely believed was enjoined by the Word of God as revealed in Scripture, and by the experience of the church. Its successor, apparently never written, was to deal with the form of civil government that similar authorities dictated. The basic argument of the first book was that the government God wants for His church is democratic: specifically that such key functions of the church as the discipline of members who stray from dogmatic standards of truth or moral standards of behavior, and the selection of the lay and clerical leaders of the church (the "elders" and "pastors" to use the terminology of the day), should be in the hands of the entire membership of each local congregation. Obviously this is a form of government that political thinkers of any period would call democratic. To call it democratic in the sixteenth century, however, was to damn it. Centuries of political thought in the Christian West on the possible varieties of government, almost always concluding that a well-ordered monarchy was clearly the variety favored if not actually required by God and by nature, had conditioned most thinking men to instinctive rejection of any form of government in which the people had much share. And this instinctive rejection could only have been fortified by the Renaissance recovery and intensive study of the classical Greek and Roman analyses of the possible forms of government and the relative advantages of each. Both traditions combined to give the very word "democracy" a distinctly negative meaning, to conjure up visions of rule by completely unprincipled and undisciplined mobs subject to no direction but that of occasional vicious and self-serving demagogues.

All of this Morely realized. He was particularly aware of the classical analyses of forms of government, above all of Aristotle's, and he saw that once the analogy between civil and ecclesiastical government was openly admitted, the classical arguments against democracy could be brought to bear against his proposal. At two points in his book he grapples directly with this problem. The first time he denies that the government he proposes is really a "democracy" in the ancient sense. The two great disadvantages of a democracy in the ancients' eyes, he says, are that it has no body of law and no mechanism of administration. Both these essential prerequisites, however, can be found in the form of church government he is supporting. Holy Scripture provides the necessary body of law. Through it God has already done the legislative work necessary to the church of defining doctrine and morals. And in it He clearly provides for the selection of a "Moderating Council . . . composed of Pastors and Elders legitimately elected," which becomes the necessary mechanism of administration.

The second time Morely raises the problem of democracy in church government, he goes even further and leans even more heavily on the principle of analogy. He goes so far as to argue that a "democracy" dominated by law is actually the best form of civil government. He points to the Athenian and Roman Republics as examples of such a government and insists that they in fact provide the models from which all that is good in contemporary civil government derives. And he bolsters this claim by noting that Aristotle observed that just as a banquet to which many bring dishes is better than one prepared by a single person, so a government taking the advice of many is better than a government controlled by few. The conclusion Morely draws from this line of reasoning, of course, is that the natural reasoning embodied in the authors of antiquity reinforces at this point the scriptural revelation that God wants church government to be democratic. It was not then to his purpose to develop further the notion that democracy was the best form of civil government. Whether he would in fact have developed that notion in his second volume probably will never be known. It would have been unusually audacious of him to have done so. And it would almost certainly have cost him the favor of the powerful Huguenot aristocrats who did for a time help him.

Since Morely would have been so vulnerable on this point, it is somewhat surprising that this part of his argument did not not draw more fire and draw it earlier. That it did not may be a demonstration that it seemed somewhat peripheral to the fundamental issues at stake in the minds of the antagonists on both sides. But it may also be owing to a tactical decision made by Morely's principal early opponent, Antoine de la Roche-Chandieu, the most prominent of the Parisian Protestant ministers, who was devoted to Calvin and Beza, and who had been charged by the Reformed synods with the task of formally refuting Morely's program. Chandieu based his refutation almost entirely upon an extended exegesis of the Biblical passages that Morely had used. He denied flatly that there could be any analogy between civil and ecclesiastical government and therefore rejected any argument about the form of ecclesiastical government drawn from secular authorities or natural reason. He charged, indeed, that argument from analogy was a fundamental source of the fallacies of Morely's entire program. Since he based so much of his attack upon this charge, he could hardly scold Morely for introducing democracy into the church and tax him with the classical arguments against that form of government. And so he avoided the subject altogether and paid no attention to Morely's statements about democracy.

When Beza turned to his public attack on Morely, however, he did not worry about such logical scruples. He did not really have to. Chandieu had prepared his reasoned and complete refutation to Morely's entire program to win back the man's supporters or any Protestants disposed to waver in France. Beza wrote his letters largely to counter the influence of Ramus abroad, in intellectual centers where the details of the controversy and Morely himself were hardly known. Beza was thoroughly Aristotelian in many aspects of his own thought and was fully aware of the classic use of the term "democracy." He could, furthermore, be quite sure that most of his correspondents, and the wider public for whom he published many of these letters, would share this background and this attitude. He therefore seized upon the charge of "democracy" as a useful polemical point to score against Morely and his party, employing it again and again. In the most extended of these letters, addressed to Henry Bullinger, leader of the Reformed Church in Zurich and the most influential contemporary Protestant leader of the Zwinglian tradition, Beza charges that Morely has called the French Reformed church government an "oligarchy" or "tyranny" and that he is trying to replace it with the "most troublesome and most seditious democracy." This particular attack had its desired effect. Bullinger replied that he had not heard of Morely before, but suspected he must belong to the dreadful sect of Anabaptists, a condemnation, which, to Bullinger, may well have been the harshest possible. He could not really believe, however, that Ramus could have held such terrible opinions.

In other letters Beza goes further in developing this line of argument. In one, which he later published, he begins by denying that the church should be "democratic" and argues that it should rather be a "monarchy," with Jesus Christ as king. He then briefly discusses the role of different orders of clergy, the possibility of "tyranny" arising within an ecclesiastical organization, and relations between clerical and civil authorities. And he returns to the problem of "democracy" by examining and refuting a number of arguments drawn from Scripture by the proponents of more democratic church government.

Throughout these letters, Beza constantly uses the classic terms for types of government in discussing his ideal of suitable church government, but is not altogether consistent in his use of these terms. Sometimes his ideal is a "monarchy" governed by Christ. At other times it is dominated by the "aristocratic" principle, embodied in the consistory. But never is it a "democracy." That term, indeed, is almost invariably coupled with a negatively weighted adjective or two, and Beza is obviously using it as a polemical weapon.

These are the most considered and extended references to "democracy" resulting from the entire controversy. They are very nearly the most complete and the earliest (of which I have knowledge) in the entire Reformation period. They make it clear that there were thinkers, in the earlier stages of the Protestant Reformation, who were quite willing to consider analogies between civil and ecclesiastical government and to apply to one sphere arguments drawn from thought about the best form of government in the other sphere. And at least one of these thinkers was convinced that a "democratic" government was best for the church, and might also be best for civil society.

Direct debate between Morely and Beza did not long survive the St. Bartholomew's massacres, for they were most savage in the very areas where Morely had won support and seem to have wiped out his faction. Beza's personal ascendancy within the French Reformed church was confirmed, and with it the synodical or "presbyterian" form of government that has persisted within that church to the present. The ideas developed during this debate, however, were to appear again in other places and at other times. In English-speaking countries, for example, similar debates were soon joined between Congregational and Presbyterian factions of the Puritan movement, and reached a climax in the 1640's, when radical Britain wrestled with the problem of the proper church polity to substitute for that of Charles I and William Laud. Several of the leading polemicists in that battle cited Morely in passing, generally disparagingly. Arguments from analogy like Beza's were used against the threat of ecclesiastical anarchy even by Congregationalists.

In an even later period, when the battle for democracy had become largely secular, Morely's name was mentioned again. It was cited by Jean-Jacques Rousseau, the unhappy Genevan who became the Enlightenment's greatest exponent of political democracy. I have found no evidence, however, that Rousseau knew of Morely's ideas. He discussed the burning of Morely's book in Geneva, but only to argue that the Genevan authorities of his day did not have a similar legal right to burn his *Social Contract*.

Perhaps further research will uncover yet more evidence of a continuing impact of this sixteenth-century French Protestant dispute. In any event, the quarrel illustrates neatly one of the many perennial problems in relations between state and church. Now we argue less about whether church democracy will lead to a disturbing political democracy, more about whether a beneficent political democracy requires democracy in the church.

III. WAS CALVIN'S THOUGHT THE INSPIRATION FOR THE EARLIEST DEMOCRATIC REVOLTS IN EUROPE?

Hans Baron

CALVINIST IDEAS OF RESISTANCE GREW FROM CIVIC EXPERIENCE

Hans Baron (b. 1900) was born in Berlin, Germany. He received his training at the Universities of Leipzig and Berlin, earning his Ph.D. in history at the latter institution in 1922. Fleeing Nazi Germany, he eventually emigrated to the United States where he has held teaching posts at several different universities. He is now The Newberry Library Distinguished Research Fellow and Professorial Lecturer in Renaissance Studies in the History Department of the University of Chicago. Although best known for his many publications on the Italian Renaissance, Baron also has maintained a deep interest in the history of political thought during the Reformation.

RECENT research on the rôle played by Calvinism in the political and economic development of modern Europe has some resemblance to the mythical fight against the Lernaean hydra. For decades historians have tried to cut off the heads of this theory, and have indeed proved that at many points in modern history Calvinist religion was practised without any of the political and economic consequences which are said to be closely connected with the Calvinist attitude towards life. Yet historians who have studied the growth of the modern world, have ascertained again and again that Calvinist countries or circles reacted in a way different from that of Catholics and Lutherans. Whenever one head of the theory had been cut, two other heads grew at once. What is the reason for this strange failure?

The main reason, it seems to me, is that all the attempts to refute the theory of particular Calvinist influences on the modern capitalistic and democratic spirit, have only shown that Calvinism did not produce the supposed effects under all circumstances and in all places. There were Calvinist countries indeed which remained economically backward and far from any capitalistic evolution, and there were Calvinist statesmen and political thinkers who were dependent in their political views more on legal or historical arguments than religious convictions. But such discoveries will hardly hit the heart of the theory. The real problem can only be whether there was in Calvinism a psychological or intellectual disposition apt to develop its historic effects whenever the environment became favorable to its evolution. We have to put the question in such a way as to ask whether the so-called Calvinist attitude appeared only occasionally, and therefore by chance, or whether this attitude can already be found at an early stage and was continued later on, if not everywhere, yet as frequently as inheritable characteristics recur among the members of a family. The first and main question must be: are we able to find some traces of the ideas, which are

From Hans Baron, "Calvinist Republicanism and its Historical Roots," *Church History*, VIII (1939), 30–41. Reprinted by permission of *Church History* and courtesy of the author.

alleged to have grown up from Calvinism in later times, in the very days when the Calvinist attitude towards life was born?

I need not say that we cannot trace the origins of Calvinist thought today without referring first of all to Martin Butzer, the great theologian, humanist, and civic leader of Strassburg. A scholar who recently tried to summarize the debt of Calvin to Butzer concluded his description with the words that Butzer was in fact "the father of Calvinism." We know today indeed that very many features of what we regard as typical of Calvinistic theology and church organization had been foreshadowed in Butzer's writings and in the institutions of the Strassburg church—from the Calvinist emphasis on the *honor* and *sovereignty* of God, and the stress on the Old Testament, to the interpretation of the New Testament as containing divine, immutable rules for the constitution of the church. Moreover, we know, or at least ought to know—because this discovery was made nearly a generation ago—that Butzer in his religious appreciation of economic activities anticipated many views of later Puritans. Let us ask today whether *political theory* can be added to all these surprising discoveries; moreover, if this be the case, how far the fact that so many Calvinist peculiarities were anticipated in the city-state of Strassburg can help to explain the sociological problems of later Calvinism.

I must, I think, make a preliminary remark about the general political situation of Europe on the eve of the Reformation. Europe at that time seemed to fall prey to the rising forces of absolutism. In the fifteenth century, monarchy had begun to build up the modern state, and all the forces which had kept monarchism within its bounds during the Middle Ages—cities, estates, and the political theories of scholasticism—were then about to lose their strength, overshadowed by that new and overwhelming phenomenon, the rise of the centralised national monarchy. In the first half of the sixteenth century, there was in France (as has been said by a French scholar) only one God, one king, one creed, and one law. Events in England, under the Tudor dynasty, took a similar direction. In Italy, the city-state, the very basis of Italian civilization during the Middle Ages, had already been defeated in its struggle against the tyranny of the Renaissance; it was losing its last freedom when the Spanish monarchy built up its hegemony over the peninsula. This Spanish monarchv was also threatening the old territorial freedom of cities as well as princes in Germany. In short, the free development of provincial and urban life, which had hitherto been characteristic of Europe, seemed doomed to be wiped out. . . .

Scholastic learning, in politics as well as in all other branches of culture, lost contact with the actual course of life during the fifteenth century. To the seventeenth and eighteenth centuries the doctrines of the sovereignty of the people and of a binding contract as the basis of government were to mean much because vital tendencies of the day were not entirely dissimilar from these doctrines. In the fifteenth and early sixteenth centuries, the driving force in the evolution of the modern state was not active participation of the citizens, but absolutism of the ruling dynasty. The doctrine advocated by late scholastic writers of a social contract based on natural law was academic theory, or a revival of classical ideas, but had little in common with reality. Natural law was losing its efficacy to influence actual life in proportion as the tide of absolutism rose. During the Middle Ages a trenchant weapon of the church in her struggles against real or alleged tyranny of secular rulers, the doctrine of natural law was without much practical value to the fifteenth and early sixteenth centuries. The Renaissance as well as the Reformation had to look for further intellectual weapons if the rising power of absolutism was to be checked.

The humanists of the Italian city-states found this weapon in a new discovery of the historical past—in a new philosophy of history. They became aware of the rôle which the city-state and the local initiative of politically minded citizens had played for antiquity, and again for the medieval cities. They revealed the destruction of civic initiative through the rise of that same universal monarchy of the emperors, which had appeared to the Middle Ages, as requested by religion and decreed by God. Even Machiavelli, who regarded a strong monarchy as the only practical help for Italy in his own day, blamed Caesar for having established permanent despotism in the world, instead of safeguarding the free development of the Roman people. In strongest contrast to the medieval ideal of a universal monarchy he claimed that "Where there are many states, there arise many efficient men; where the states are few, the efficient men are rare."

It was precisely this same problem—the problem of the preservation of civic initiative and regional independence—that faced the world of the Reformation, north of the Alps. The city-state of the Italian Renaissance had been doomed in the end. Of Machiavelli's literary work, only his guide for the tyrant who would unite the peninsula was read and appreciated. The extent to which the old political variety of Europe with its gradation of freedom and intiative would be preserved practically depended upon the Reformation.

For Protestantism, this question was a vital problem. All the great monarchs, who were the overlords of Spain and Italy, of France and Germany, of Scotland and of the Netherlands, and to a certain extent even the English kings, became close allies of re-invigorated Catholicism. Complete victory of the absolute monarchy would have meant extinction of the Reformation movement everywhere. The starting-points for the new religion, on the other hand, were individual local circles—estates, cities, provinces (like the Netherlands), or sections of the civic element and the nobility. A natural alliance was to link the Reformation with the political opponents of centralising absolutism. The political struggle of the cities and estates for the defence of their liberty gained a new background, a higher motive, in the defence of religion.

In practice, however, this alliance could only be achieved by means of painstaking political and intellectual work. Luther's religious outlook on life contained no tonic to political aspirations. Natural law with its weapons against "tyranny" meant to Luther as little as it did to the humanists. To Luther the whole scholastic tradition of natural law was one of those pernicious mixtures of spiritual religion and the worldly sphere, which the new faith was to dissolve. If a king asks his officials or subject authorities to act against true religion, he must be opposed through disobedience and passive resistance. Whoever ascribes to religion any further demands, vitiates religion. In the political sphere, the duty of the Christian is to accept and revere existing conditions as created by God. A king who has been admitted to his throne can never rightly be opposed by any subject, without regard to whether territorial authorities or ordinary private citizens feel impelled to defend religion by the force of arms.

The consequences of this attitude of the German Reformer for the history of the Empire are well known. After all, Protestantism was defended. In the decisive hour, the constitution of the Empire was interpreted as being a federation of sovereign princes who, according to positive constitutional law, were entitled to resist religious encroachments on the part of an overlord whom they themselves, through the intervention of the Electors, had elected. In this way Protestantism was saved in Germany, but the absolute power of the Hapsburg emperor was replaced by the territorial absolutism of many Protestant as well as Catholic princes.

This princely interpretation of the constitution of the Empire, however, did not benefit the imperial cities. According to positive law, they were mere subjects of the emperor. Subordinated as they were to a Catholic lord, they could have no hope in matters of religion, unless they succeeded in making local self-government politically victorious against the rise of the centralising monarchy—unless they were able to check absolutism in the name of religion. Thus, an historic hour came for the civic element. In urban surroundings the Reformation was to take a political turn. Of Nuremberg and Strassburg, the old leaders of the German cities, Strassburg took the first place, as economically the most self-sufficient and politically the most uncompromising of the German city-states. In Strassburg, therefore, must be sought the first amalgamation of Protestantism with new political ideas. With this we are led back to Butzer, Strassburg's leading theologian.

At the end of the 1520's, when it became clear that Charles V had definitely decided to suppress Protestantism throughout the Empire, Butzer took up the grave problem of resistance in his commentary on St. Matthew. He did not depart from Luther's view that the Christian has to regard existing law and conditions as willed by God. But in the hands of this citizen of Strassburg the same maxim was capable of creating opposite results. As the actual outcome of history, Butzer said, is the existence of *magistratus inferiores* everywhere, of self-governing city-authorities as well as of territorial princes, the demand of religion to preserve the order established by God implies the careful conservation of this political variety. Whether good or bad, whether legally guaranteed or not, the fact is that a gradation in the political world has been created by history. An overlord who would try to limit by force the functions of these minor powers, would thereby act against the will of God.

Viewed in this light, the inferior authorities gained a new dignity, a new spiritual strength. In their small sphere, they appeared as not less responsible for the religious welfare of their subjects than the overlord in his vast kingdom. They must resist encroachments of their superior upon their political rights, because loss of freedom might pave the way for the suppression of religion. Minor authorities must remember, Butzer said in an impressive word, that it remains their highest duty to beautify the "Sparta" which has been given to them by God.

Thus religion and politics were establishing a new alliance. Only religion, in Butzer's view, can explain and justify the fact that history has preserved this wealth of minor authorities. The early Jewish state of the Old Testament was evidence to him that God does not approve of unlimited absolutism. Like the humanists, Butzer did not reflect on any inviolable rights sanctioned by nature. The gravest argument for him lay with history. Italian humanists had gone back from imperial Rome, the birthplace of the universal empire of the Middle Ages, to the *Republica Romana,* the state of a free people. The civic theologian of Strassburg went back from David's kingdom, the foreshadowing of the spiritual kingdom of Christ, to the early Jewish state, the state of a free people. God himself, Butzer said, declared that He gave His people a king in Saul only in His wrath. Moses, before that time, had shared his power with many judges and with his priestly brother; although the leader of his people, he was more the servant of all than their prince. Those who have championed a universal monarchy, have dreamt of a world which has never existed, and which no well-meaning man should desire. A mortal man is not capable of governing one single town in a perfect way. To concentrate in an individual the power of the world, would mean to destroy the gradation of the world willed by God. As Butzer expressed it later in his *Lectures on the Book of Judges:* "Wherever absolute power is given to a prince, there the glory and the dominion of God is injured. The absolute power, which is God's alone, would be given to a man liable to sin."

Butzer would not have ventured this opposition to monarchy merely for political reasons. A contemporary of Machiavelli, he held a high opinion of the political benefits of centralizing all initiative in a single hand. He pointed out with emphasis that even the Roman republic knew dictatorial concentration of power in the hour of need. It was the consequence of his *religious* thought which drove him further along the path of constitutional and even republican ideas. If absolute power of a prince impairs the sovereignty of God, then legal provisions to call a prince to account in an emergency are a demand of *religion.* Moreover, the very basis of monarchy, heredity, becomes suspect from the religious point of view. In a hereditary kingdom, the judgment of God is prejudiced. There ought to be room for divine selection of those whom God will place at the helm of the state, and whom He benefits with the spirit of His wisdom. *Elective* monarchy, and not a hereditary kingdom, is the constitution favored by religion. This, stated Butzer, would be the ideal order of a state: either one or a few men would have the power; but these men ought to be designated by God. They would govern on the basis of a legal order. Absolute power would not be conferred on any ruler.

The direct successor to this whole mode of thought was Calvin. It was his task to translate the German constitutional conceptions of Butzer into the legal language of the western European countries. In western Europe the backbone of resistance to the rising wave of absolutism was not local self-government of city-states and territorial princes, but the participation of the estates (the *Etats Généraux* in France) in the central government, if only on a few traditional occasions. In Calvin's *Institutio Christiana* the place of Butzer's *magistratus inferiores,* that is, the leaders of local self-administration, is therefore taken by the *magistratus populares,* the *ephors* of the people, the estates general.

Starting from this basis, Calvin went beyond Butzer's teachings by filling them with unparalleled energy and unique logical consistency. But in purport he only increased and brought to maturity what Butzer had initiated. In the famous passages of the *Institutio Christiana* on political constitution and resistance, the *leit-motif* was (as it had been for Butzer) an attempt to transform Luther's claim for reverence for the existing political conditions into a measure of defence for the existing minor authorities as sanctioned by the course of history. In the last edition of the *Institutio* (in 1559), and in his sermons and commentaries on the Bible at that time, Calvin drew from these convictions the same political conclusions which Butzer had once drawn. If preservation of the *sovereignty* of God in earthly life is in the centre of religion, assignment of unlimited power to a mortal creature is an offence against God. Legal limitations upon the ruler are required by *religion.* And in the final judgment, heredity of the throne impairs divine selection of the ruler and is therefore inferior to any form of elective government.

The growth of these republican tendencies in Calvin's thought during his later years has frequently been regarded as a mere reflection of local experience at Geneva and the suppression of the Reformation through the royal power in France. Yet one can observe with philological precision that the preceding experience of Butzer in the Strassburg city-state played no less a part for Calvin, and co-operated in the formation of his political ideas as a decisive factor. Butzer's *Lectures on the Book of Judges,* which had raised the first plain criticism at monarchy from a religious view-point, were published as a posthumous work in 1554, in the Geneva of Calvin. It was from the following year onwards that the pronounced expressions of an antimonarchic attitude appeared in Calvin's works—partly in almost literal conformity with Butzer's arguments.

If a clear-cut definition is desired, it might be best to say that Calvinist Geneva was the first historical *application* of Calvinist political theory, but that the city-state of Strassburg, a generation earlier, had offered the soil on which this theory had *grown.* This definition has the advantage that it reminds us of the crucial point: what we know as the political doctrine of Calvin and so many of his followers had been the product of an historic co-operation of Protestant religion and the civic world of the city-state. The new outlook on politics in a religious guise had been older than Calvin. It had originated at the very moment when the civic element of the Renaissance period and the new religion had joined forces for the first time.

This broad sociological background

alone is sufficient to account for the enormous influence of Calvinist political ideas during several centuries to come. To the Calvinist thinkers of the second half of the sixteenth century, however aggressive these *Monarchomachi* were, the old theories of a social contract and of the sovereignty of the people, based on natural law, remained without vital importance, or were at least merely a supplement to the dominating religious and biblical conceptions. Catholic opponents were often more prepared to lay decisive stress on the old claim of the natural rights of the people. Yet Calvinist political thought helped more than any other tendency of the time to prevent a full victory of absolutism, and to prepare the way for constitutional and even republican ideas.

H. G. Koenigsberger

CALVINISTS AND CATHOLICS BOTH ORGANIZE REVOLUTIONARY PARTIES

H. G. Koenigsberger (b. 1918) was born in Berlin, Germany, but reared and educated in England. He took his training in history at Gonville and Caius College, Cambridge. After serving in the Royal Navy in World War II, he taught at the University of Manchester and later at the University of Nottingham. He was also a visiting lecturer at a number of American universities. Since 1966 he has been Professor of Early Modern European History at Cornell University where he teaches courses in Renaissance, Reformation, and sixteenth-century Spanish and Dutch history. He has been secretary of the International Commission for the History of Representative and Parliamentary Institutions since 1955. His latest book, published in 1968 and written with George L. Mosse, is entitled *Europe in the Sixteenth Century.*

IT is a commonplace of modern historical writing that the sixteenth century was the age of "new monarchies" in western Europe. The establishment of centralized government and capitalist finance, the introduction of Roman law and of professional civil servants, have been extensively studied; the work of Habsburg, Valois, and Tudor rulers in unifying great kingdoms is well known. Not so well known is the nature of the oppositions which the governments of the sixteenth century had to face. Too often these oppositions have been represented as the survivals of the old feudal nobility fighting a rear-guard action for their medieval privileges, or as the first stirrings of the "rising middle classes," staking a claim for religious liberty and a more active citizenship against monarchial despotism. It is true that some historians have described the organization of sixteenth-century oppositions and have appreciated that their revolutionary activities were possible only through the efforts of a highly developed party organization. The present essay attempts to show that these organizations were not isolated phenomena, but rather the logical counterpart of the increased power of the state; that they were nearly always the result of the efforts of determined minorities who tried to impose their views on the country by force; that without such organization these minorities could not hope to succeed; and that

From H. G. Koenigsberger, "The Organization of Revolutionary Parties in France and the Netherlands during the Sixteenth Century," *The Journal of Modern History,* XXVII (1955), 335–340, 345–351. Reprinted by permission of the author and *The Journal of Modern History.*

they did succeed only where the government was temporarily weak. If the origins of the organization of the modern state can be found in the monarchies of Francis I, Henry VIII, and Philip II, the origins of the organization of the Jacobins and of the totalitarian parties of the twentieth century can be found in the Huguenots and Holy League of France, the Water Beggars and Calvinists of the Netherlands and, to a lesser degree, in Knox's "brethren" and the Lords of the Congregation of Scotland.

European governments had been faced with oppositions before the sixteenth century. These oppositions had nearly always been limited to one class, or group of classes, as in the medieval peasant revolts and in feudal movements such as the League of the Common Weal in France; or they had been revolts on a limited territorial basis. In the sixteenth century, almost for the first time, opposition movements became nation wide and included classes, or elements of classes, ranging from princes of the blood to unemployed artisans. These opposition movements might act through a parliament or assembly of estates, or —and this happened to all of them at some time in their careers— they could become openly revolutionary. It is only this revolutionary aspect of sixteenth-century oppositions which will be discussed in this article.

The new factor which made possible these formidable parties was religion. Religious belief alone, no matter whether it was held with fanatic conviction or for political expediency, could bring together the divergent interests of nobles, burghers, and peasants over areas as wide as the whole of France. And it was religious organizations from which developed the organization of political parties or which provided the prototype for party organization. "It is common knowledge, confirmed by many examples," wrote the Venetian ambassador to France in 1561, "that, with a change of religion, there will of necessity follow changes of states" (i.e., revolutions).

France, the classical land of revolutions, provided two of the sixteenth-century revolutionary movements, the Huguenots and the League. The transformation of the scattered Calvinist communities into the highly organized Huguenot party, capable of surviving a generation of civil wars, was the answer to the attempts of Henry II to exterminate heresy through the machinery of the state. The initiative in this response was taken not only by the French Calvinists, but by Calvin himself, in Geneva. The Huguenot movement had, therefore, from its beginnings the characteristics of an international, as well as of a national, party. Wherever a Protestant community was established it elected its elders and deacons to assure the discipline of the faithful, administer the funds of the community, and, in general, look after the physical and spiritual welfare of its members. In the larger towns the organization was more elaborate, with the election of *quarteniers*, *centeniers*, and *dizeniers*. The pastors of the larger communities, or of groups of smaller ones, were often appointed by Theodore Beza or by Calvin himself; thus spiritual control was centralized in Geneva.

As the Protestant communities grew and attracted persons from an ever wider range of classes, secret conventicles changed into open mass meetings. By 1557 assemblies of two or three thousand in the Cévennes offered armed resistance to the king's officials who sought to prevent the scandal of the public preaching of heresy. From the end of 1559 such events became common over the greater part of France. The new doctrines had appealed, at first, to the small artisans and shopkeepers and to the unemployed workers and journeymen of the towns, all of them hit by rising prices, heavy wartime taxation, and the growing influence and rigidity of the guilds which blocked economic advance to all but the favored few. To them the eloquence of the Geneva-trained preachers brought a message of hope and hate that the local curé could not hope to emulate. At the same time, many of the richer bourgeoisie and the professional classes, and more especially their womenfolk, were drawn towards the new doctrines. Disgust with the generally admitted abuses of the old church, the half-understood or misinterpreted Calvinist doctrine of the lawfulness of usury, or, simply, the hope of gain from the vast wealth of the church—these were the powerful inducements that made men accept protestantism. After the end of the war with Spain, large numbers of the nobility, especially the impoverished lower nobility of the south, began to join the new movement for a similar variety of reasons.

Two results followed immediately upon this marriage of social and religious forces. Within the short period of about two years, from the end of 1559 to the beginning of 1562, the majority of the Calvinist communities placed themselves under the protection of a local seigneur. His influence would bring new converts, especially from the country population which had been comparatively untouched by the new religion. The price revolution of the sixteenth century had tended to benefit the French peasant and left him reasonably well contented with his lot; with the natural conservatism of the countryman he was averse to changes in religion. The best chance for the reformers to make headway among the peasantry was, therefore, to act through the local country gentlemen whose change of religion the peasant on his estate would be obliged to follow. But even more important was the military element introduced by the nobility. The conventicles became military cadres; mass meetings of armed men, protected by the local nobility and their retainers, began to invade the churches to celebrate their services in open defiance of public authority and of the majority of the Catholic population. Nor did this happen only in the south. In May 1560, their assemblies in Rouen were said to be 20,000 strong. The royal commander, with 5,000 troops, could not prevent the scaffolds and gibbets he had set up from being pulled down again and he did not dare to take further action.

The Huguenot military cadres were now organized on a provincial and national basis in the same way as the religious communities already had been organized in their provincial and national synods. The synod of Clairac, in November 1560, divided the province of Guienne into seven *colloques*, each with its captain. In 1561 the synod of Sainte-Foy decided on the election of two "protectors," one for the region of Toulouse and one for that of Bordeaux. Under them were the colonels of the *colloques* and under these the captains of the individual communities, each strictly responsible to his immediate superior. When the first civil war broke out, in 1562, this organization was more or less fully developed in Guienne, Languedoc, Provence, and Dauphiné, and it existed at least in outline in the rest of France. As the government sought to break Calvinism by increasingly severe edicts and official persecution, the Calvinist communities came to rely more and more on their noble patrons and their military organization. Inevitably, the control of the movement tended to shift from the preachers to the nobles, despite Calvin's misgivings and his efforts to prevent it.

Now it only remained for the movement to find a leader among the higher nobility. When Condé took the title of protector-general of the churches of France all the enormous influence of the Bourbon connection was added to the Huguenot party. The combination of feudal power with the military organization of the Calvinist communities, the financial backing of wealthy bankers and merchants, the voluntary contributions of the faithful, the religious faith kept aflame by skillful propaganda and organized in a strict communal discipline that held together in a common purpose social groups with basically divergent outlooks and interests—all these provided Condé with a political instrument such as no "overmighty subject" had disposed of before. The international organization of Christian communities which Calvin had built up and controlled from Geneva had become a national French revolutionary movement. It never broke with its international connection; it could still obtain material aid from Protestant England

and Calvinist Palatinate; it supported William of Orange and provided the Water Beggars with a base of operations at La Rochelle; its preachers still looked to Geneva for spiritual guidance; but all its energies, its hopes and aims, were now concentrated on France.

Nevertheless, this organization could not have been built up if it had not been for the weakness of the government after the death of Henry II. Local Catholic officials and magistrates were halfhearted in the execution of the king's edicts and, after his death, were less inclined than ever to visit the full rigor of the law on their Huguenot neighbors and countrymen. Many officials, moreover, secretly sympathized with the Huguenots or had frankly joined the movement. Throughout the years 1560 and 1561 the Vicomte de Joyeuse, acting governor of Languedoc, wrote to the king and to the constable, Montmorency, painting in ever darker colors his waning authority, the unreliability of his officials, and the increasing power and influence of the Huguenots who added insult to injury by claiming to act in the king's name. Worst of all, the central government itself failed to back its provincial governors. While Guises, Bourbons, and Montmorencys were maneuvering for position and Catherine de Medici was trying to prevent any one of the factions from becoming too powerful, no consistent policy could be maintained. "I never sawe state more amased than this at somtyme, and by and by more reckless," the English ambassador reported from the court at Amboise; "they know not whome to mistruste, nor to truste. This day they licence som to departe: to morrowe they revoke theym. He hath all the trust this daye, that tomorrow is leste trusted."

In sharp contrast to the vacillation of the court were the determined actions of the Huguenot party. In October 1561 they seized Montauban and a number of smaller towns around Toulouse. Once established in any town they acted with great ruthlessness to carry out their aims and maintain themselves in power. They plundered churches and committed them to their preachers; they sacked monasteries, chased away the monks, and forcibly married off the nuns. Joyeuse reported that even good Catholics were so terrorized by the Huguenot mob that there was not a clerk who would write, nor a witness who would testify, against them. In the course of the first two civil wars the movement took over the government's financial machinery in the provinces they controlled, imposed taxes on both Protestants and Catholics, prevented all payments to the Catholic church and to the government, and even struck coins with Condé's image. Where they could not dominate a region completely, they infiltrated into public offices, until there was a Huguenot hierarchy of officials intermingled with the royal administration and owing allegiance not to the king but to Condé and Coligny. "Thus," said the Venetian ambassador in 1569, "they could, in one day, at one definite hour, and with all secrecy start a rising in every part of the kingdom and unleash a cruel and perilous war."

The organization of the Huguenot movement reached its fullest development only after the Massacre of St. Bartholomew, and its survival after that terrible blow was, in itself, evidence of its strength. But in the later stages of the civil wars it gradually lost much of its revolutionary ardor. By 1588 the Duke of Nevers—a very astute observer—thought that the Huguenots had had their fling and that they were now on the defensive: whole provinces and towns were no longer joining them, he wrote. Where they were not forced to do otherwise, the vast majority of Frenchmen preferred to remain loyal to the old faith. Even the succession to the crown of France of the Huguenot leader Henry of Navarre could not alter this fact. But it did save France from the fate of the Netherlands: permanent division. Thanks to their military organization the Huguenots became the "state within the state," an organization beyond the control of the central government but bent no longer on its overthrow. . . .

It is not surprising that Calvinist extremism should have evoked the reaction of a similar Catholic extremism. In the Netherlands the Spanish government itself represented Catholic extremism. Independent Catholic organization, as in the Union of Arras, was therefore largely conservative and nonrevolutionary. In France, however, the Catholic government was weak and willing to compromise with the Huguenots. Local Catholic unions, or leagues, therefore began to be formed by local authorities, nobles, and prelates as early as 1560 and 1562, especially in the south where Huguenot pressure was at its strongest. But it was only in 1576, after Henry III's far-reaching concessions to the Huguenots in the Peace of Monsieur, that the local leagues were organized into a nation-wide league, or holy union. Where the Huguenot party had been built on the union of the militarized Calvinist communities with the Bourbon family connection, the League was built on the union of the military Catholic nobility with the Guise family connection. Where the Huguenots and the Water Beggars looked to Geneva for spiritual guidance and to England and the Protestant princes of Germany for material help, the Leaguers looked to Rome and to the Catholic rulers of Spain and Savoy. Thus, all three revolutionary movements were linked with powers and interests outside their national boundaries. This added to their strength, but it also set up tensions within the movements that greatly increased the difficulties of unified leadership.

The League of 1576 was founded as a Catholic party of the nobility with essentially conservative aims: Henry III and his successors were to be preserved in their authority according to their coronation oaths and without prejudice to the estates; the provinces were to have their ancient rights restored to them. This program did not differ substantially from many similar feudal programs of the middle ages. But the remaining nine articles had a most unmedieval ring; they were the articles dealing with the organization of the League. All members were to defend each other, by force of arms if need be; the governors of towns and villages were secretly to advise Catholics to join the association and to provide arms and men according to their faculties; all were to swear prompt and strict obedience to the chief of the League, without respect for any other authority; all who refused to join were to be regarded as enemies and those who, having joined, wanted to withdraw were to be effectively outlawed and hounded down while their pursuers would be protected from all public and private reprisals. A powerful religious sanction was provided by the oath which every member had to take, binding himself to observe the articles on pain of anathema and eternal damnation.

In many parts of France the League was broadened to include the clergy and the *tiers état* and, just as in the Huguenot movement, the lower orders were enrolled to provide mass support.

Th power of this new party became immediately apparent in the States General of Blois in 1576. The agents of the League were everywhere. They manipulated the elections and intimidated voters; League *baillis* and *sénéchaux* tried to prevent the Huguenots from attending the electoral meetings. Within the assembly they organized an adroit attack on the king's powers in the name of the old privileges of the estates and provinces.

For all its formidable organization, however, the League was not yet a revolutionary party. But as a threat to the king's independence it was too dangerous to be ignored, the more so, as its close links with Madrid were well known. To draw its teeth, therefore, and if possible to make it serve his own purposes by providing troops and money against the Protestants, Henry III declared himself chief of the League in January 1577. As head of such an organization he hoped to have far greater powers and authority over his subjects than he had ever had as king. But, as the Duke of Nevers pointed out immediately, the nobility were not likely to exchange their vague obligations to serve the king for the very precise and far-reaching obligations they would have to the king as chief of the League. The organization which had been created to coerce the king disintegrated in his hands when he tried to use it for his own purposes. If this was disappointing, it was still better than leaving such a weapon in the hands of the Duke of Guise. In the Peace of Bergerac, in September 1577, all leagues and associations were dissolved by royal edict.

The League of 1576 had been dominated by the nobility and its aims had been primarily constitutional. Until the king's interference unified control by the Duke of Guise had been comparatively easy. The League which appeared in 1585, after the death of the Duke of Anjou had revealed to Catholics the specter of a Protestant succession, was at once more revolutionary and much less homogeneous. It started as a secret society of a small number of fanatical Catholics among the Parisian bourgeoisie, mostly priests and professional men. Its discipline, dedication to the cause and puritanical insistence on the personal virtue of its members, was as severe as in any Calvinist community. When they had built up a strong party among the artisans, guilds, and public officials of the municipality they entered into relations with Guise and the Catholic princes. Immediately, the old League of 1576 reappeared all over France. In town after town the Leaguers removed royalist commanders and governors and replaced them by their own men, on the pretext of insuring a firmer anti-Huguenot policy. Not for the last time, a moderate government fighting a revolutionary party found itself outbid by an extremist and equally revolutionary party on its own side.

In Paris, the League rapidly gained in strength and confidence. Their growing tyranny over the city has been brilliantly traced in the diary of Pierre de l'Estoile, their bitter enemy. The Paris mob, which had already proved its talent for murderous pogroms in the Massacre of St. Bartholomew, was being systematically roused by the League preachers —for once the oratorical equals of their Calvinist rivals—until every misfortune and every crime was attributed to the Calvinists and *Politiques*. The famous "Day of the Barricades," May 12, 1588, when Henry III and his Swiss mercenaries were driven out of the capital had been planned and organized as much as a year before.

Once again, it was the weakness of the government which made possible the rapid progress of the League; for the League, again like other revolutionary parties, was only a small minority, achieving its aims by strict organization, ruthless determination of aim, and the tactics of infiltration into public offices.

After the murder of the Duke of Guise, on December 23, 1588, the League came out in open rebellion against the king. In Provence the parlement declared for the League and the towns renounced their allegiance to "the assassin Henry III."

Elsewhere it needed the appearance of Leaguer troops to overawe the loyalist provincial parlements. In almost every town the League had a strong party in the council and among the *échevins*. Members of the League now swore allegiance to Mayenne. With the help of his troops, or with the force provided by the retainers of the local Leaguer nobility, revolutionary governments were set up in almost all towns outside the Loire valley which the king managed to hold. Secret or open League committees, composed of members of the three estates, supervised the councils and imprisoned nobles and officials suspected of royalist sympathies. In Toulouse, always fanatically Catholic, the *capitouls* (mayor and corporation) declared for the League, and when the parlement wanted to maintain the king's authority, the mob invaded the court and murdered the president-general.

But it was in Paris that the revolution was carried to its furthest extremes. The League organization in each of the sixteen quarters of the city set up a committee charged with police functions and the supervision of the municipal officials. These committees, in turn, formed a central committee, called the Sixteen, after the number of quarters in the capital, but with an actual membership of up to fifty. The Sixteen established the first revolutionary reign of terror that Paris was to experience. To coordinate the movement in the provinces the Sixteen sent their agents to the provinces and received those of the provincial towns. The general council of the League was thus in full control of the whole network of Leaguer towns in France.

The aristocratic members of the general council, however, were becoming increasingly uneasy about the revolutionary and democratic policy of the Sixteen. L'Estoile was not alone in resenting the appointment of "small tradesmen and a bunch of Leaguer scoundrels" to the captaincies of the citizen guards and to high municipal offices. Already in February 1589, Mayenne had tried to counterbalance the democratic wing of the general council by appointing to it fourteen members of the Parisian *haute bourgeoisie* and the parlement. The Sixteen answered by setting up a Committee of Public Safety with ten members. In November 1591, they struck against their most hated enemy in Paris, the parlement. Brisson, its president, and the councilors Larcher and Tardif were arrested and executed for alleged treason.

This act made the breach between the aristocratic *Politiques* and the democratic Sixteen irreconcilable. In December 1591 Mayenne arrested several of the Sixteen. Others who were implicated in the execution of the Councilors fled. But Mayenne refused to act against the preachers or to destroy the Sixteen completely. Yet his attempt to hold together and balance the revolutionary and aristocratic wings of the League was doomed to failure just as the similar attempts of the Prince of Orange in the parallel situation in Flanders and Brabant, ten years before. While Henry IV steadily advanced, Mercœur and others of the high nobility, maneuvered to rescue private empires from the approaching defeat. The lower nobility began to play for safety by placing a son in each of the opposing camps. When Henry IV became a Catholic, the only effective bond between the different sections of the League, fear of a heretic king, disappeared. With the desertion of the *Politiques* and the mass of the lower nobility, the League broke up: Mayenne's ambition was left face to face with the Catholic fanaticism of the Parisian democracy. Besieged, and isolated from the provinces, their interurban contacts broken by Mayenne's intrigues and Henry's advance, their position in the capital undermined by Mayenne's "Thermidor" of 1591, the revolutionary leaders of Paris were left with only one ally —the Catholic autocrat, Philip II of Spain. It was the *reductio ad absurdum* of revolution and it was its end. The Spanish armies failed to relieve Paris, and on March 22, 1594, Henry IV entered his capital almost unopposed.

It was the paradox of the revolutionary movements of the sixteenth century that they were led by men who were not revolutionaries. Condé and Navarre, Orange, Guise and Mayenne did not create the organization of their parties. Their aim, as that of many aristocratic rebels before them, was to capture the existing machinery of state without subverting the social order or radically changing the political, or even religious, structure of the country. Yet they found themselves carried far along the path to political and social revolution by the revolutionary parties of which they were the leaders. The lower nobility who formed the most active elements in all three movements as well as their military cadres, the rich burghers and impoverished artisans of the citizen guards in the towns—these were the revolutionary forces, and they were effectively revolutionary by virtue of their economic ambitions and their religious beliefs. Religion was the binding force that held together the divergent interests of the different classes and provided them with an organization and a propaganda machine capable of creating the first genuinely national and international parties in modern European history; for these parties never embraced more than a minority of each of their constituent classes. Moreover it was through religion that they could appeal to the lowest classes and the mob to vent the anger of their poverty and the despair of their unemployment in barbarous massacres and fanatical looting. Social and economic discontent were fertile ground for recruitment by either side, and popular democratic tyranny appeared both in Calvinist Ghent and Catholic Paris.

In the long run, not even religion was able to reconcile the nobility with democratic dictatorships, and one side or the other was driven into alliance with the formerly common enemy. The result was, in every case, the breakup of the revolutionary party and the defeat of the popular movement. Where the nobility and urban patriciate managed to maintain control over the revolutionary movement they also managed to achieve a great part of their revolutionary aims. Significantly, however, the Huguenots and the Dutch Calvinists, once firmly in the saddle, abandoned the greater part of their revolutionary organization. Only in the field of religion did they carry their revolutions to the full conclusion. The Huguenots maintained their religious rights for another hundred years while the Dutch Calvinists succeeded in converting the majority of the population. Yet, in neither case did the radical wing of the Calvinists succeed in establishing a rigorous theocracy on the Geneva model. Despite the constant insistence of religious unity, the possibilities of the political single-party state were not yet fully recognized. Henry III's tentative moves in that direction ended in complete failure. A Calvinist (or Catholic) theocracy had come to be equated with democratic tyranny, and neither nobility nor urban patriciate were willing to accept this. The traditional governments, when firmly led, were still too powerful and commanded the traditional allegiance of the subject. The traditional social and political structure of Europe had still too much toughness, the traditional ruling classes still too much vitality. It was another two hundred years before they were effectively challenged and before a revolutionary party appeared that was as highly organized as those of the sixteenth century.

Michael Walzer

CALVINISTS BECOME REVOLUTIONARIES

Michael Walzer (b. 1935) is a native of New York City who earned his undergraduate degree at Brandeis University in 1956 and his doctorate at Harvard University in 1961. While a graduate student at Harvard, he spent two years in England at Cambridge University as a Fulbright Fellow. He taught at Princeton University before returning to Harvard in 1966 as an Associate Professor of Government. Walzer's commitment to research in the history of political theory and practice is reflected in his many contributions to scholarly journals and his books. He is also a member of the editorial board and frequent contributor to the journal *Dissent*.

THE study of modern politics might begin at many points in the sixteenth century: with Machiavelli and the new political realism, with Luther and the German princes and their attack upon Roman internationalism, with Bodin and the sovereignty of the new monarchs. The concern of this essay, however, is not with reason of state, the national church, or the idea of sover-

From Michael Walzer, *The Revolution of the Saints* (Cambridge, Massachusetts: Harvard University Press, 1965), pp. 1–4, 9–13, 20–21, 301–303, 312–316. Reprinted by permission of the Harvard University Press and courtesy of the author.

eignty. It lies instead with another of those startling innovations of sixteenth-century political history: the appearance of revolutionary organization and radical ideology. Revolution as a political phenomenon and ideology as a kind of mental and moral discipline are both, of course, closely related to the rise of the modern state. Yet the idea that specially designated and organized bands of men might play a creative part in the political world, destroying the established order and reconstructing society according to the Word of God or the plans of their fellows—this idea did not enter at all into the thought of Machiavelli, Luther, or Bodin. In establishing the state, these three writers relied exclusively upon the prince, whether they imagined him as an adventurer, a Christian magistrate, or a hereditary bureaucrat. All other men remained subjects, condemned to political passivity. But this was an incomplete vision, for in fact the revolutionary activity of saints and citizens played as important a part in the formation of the modern state as did the sovereign power of princes. In Switzerland, the Dutch Netherlands, Scotland, and most importantly in England and later in France, the old order was finally overthrown not by absolutist kings or in the name of reason of state but by groups of political radicals, themselves moved by new and revolutionary ideologies.

It will be argued below that it was the Calvinists who first switched the emphasis of political thought from the prince to the saint (or the band of saints) and then constructed a theoretical justification for independent political action. What Calvinists said of the saint, other men would later say of the citizen: the same sense of civic virtue, of discipline and duty, lies behind the two names. Saint and citizen together suggest a new integration of private men (or rather, of *chosen* groups of private men, of proven holiness and virtue) into the political order, an integration based upon a novel view of politics as a kind of conscientious and continuous labor. This is surely the most significant outcome of the Calvinist theory of worldly activity, preceding in time any infusion of religious worldliness into the economic order. The diligent activism of the saints—Genevan, Huguenot, Dutch, Scottish, and Puritan—marked the transformation of politics into work and revealed for the first time the extraordinary conscience that directed the work.

Conscience and work entered the political world together; they formed the basis for the new politics of revolution and shaped the character of the revolutionary. They also provided, it should be said, an internal rationale for the diligent efficiency of the modern official and the pious political concern of the modern bourgeois. But both these eminent men were revolutionaries in their time; they had first of all to construct a world in which their efficiency and concern would be respectable—and to attack an older world that had made them both objects of mockery or disdain. In politics as in religion the saints were oppositional men and their primary task was the destruction of traditional order. But they were committed after that to the literal reforming of human society, to the creation of a Holy Commonwealth in which conscientious activity would be encouraged and even required. The saints saw themselves as divine *instruments* and theirs was the politics of wreckers, architects, and builders—hard at work upon the political world. They refused to recognize any inherent or natural resistance to their labors. They treated every obstacle as another example of the devil's resourcefulness and they summoned all their energy, imagination, and craft to overcome it. Because their work required cooperation, they organized to carry it through successfully and they joined forces with any man who might help them without regard to the older bonds of family and neighborhood. They sought "brethren" and turned away if necessary from their relatives; they sought zeal and not affection. Thus there arose the leagues and covenants, the conferences and congregations which are the prototypes of revolutionary discipline. In these the good work was carried forward; at the same time, new saints were trained and hardened for their unremitting labor. The results of that labor can best be seen in the English Revolution of 1640.

In Elizabethan and Jacobean drama the Calvinist saints who later played such a crucial part in that revolution were described as men of hypocritical zeal, meddlesome, continually on the move, nervously and ostentatiously searching for godly things to do—thus Ben Jonson's Puritan, Zeal-of-the-Land Busy. Zeal-of-the-Land was a comic figure, but he was also a new man, especially susceptible to caricature. The saint's personality was his own most radical innovation. It was marked above all by an uncompromising and sustained commitment to a political ideal (which other men called hypocrisy), and by a pattern of rigorous and systematic labor in pursuit of that ideal (which other men called meddlesomeness). The origins and consequences of this godly commitment and this godly business will be examined below. It is necessary first to suggest how new both were in the sixteenth century, with what incomprehension the contemporaries of Calvin and then of Cromwell approached the savage struggles into which godly zeal and business plunged them, how frequently they doubted the "sincerity" of the saint—long after he had, one would have thought, sufficiently demonstrated it. In discussing rebellion and sedition, for example, both Bodin and Francis Bacon still thought in terms of the ragged plebeians of the classical cities and the "overmighty subjects" of bastard feudalism. Bacon, perhaps, had some foreboding of what was to come in England when he wrote a warning against unemployed scholars; such men would indeed become, though not merely because they were unemployed, the alienated intellectuals who fed the minds of the lay saints. But King James' Lord Chancellor had no sense of what this intellectual food would be like or of its consequences in human behavior. Even the great Clarendon, writing after the event, still saw the English Revolution as a conspiracy of discontented noblemen. He barely noticed the Puritans and examined their faith only as a species of hypocrisy and an excuse for "turbulence." Clarendon was very wrong; yet his opinions surely reflected the wisdom of the ages. The active, ideologically committed political radical had never before been known in Europe. Medieval society was, to use the word of a modern theorist, a society largely composed of *nonparticipants*, inactive men. A brief glance at the history of that society will suggest the novelty of Calvinist politics. . .

Machiavelli's adventurer-prince is one of the first of the "masterless men" of the sixteenth and seventeenth centuries. These were the heroes and villains of the age, cut loose from organic, hierarchical, and particularistic ties—ambitious, calculating, irreverent—insensitive to the ancient mysteries but not yet integrated into a modern social system. Some of these men eventually found a new master in Calvin's God and then they set to work creating a new society in which he could be glorified and they could be active. Calvin pursued power in Geneva with all the artfulness of a Machiavellian adventurer; the same might be said of his followers in England. Yet the elements of seventeenth-century revolutionary politics need only be listed to suggest the distance the English Calvinists had come not only from the passivity of medieval members, but also from the pure self-aggrandizement of Renaissance princes.

First, the judicial murder—and not the assassination—of King Charles I; the trial of the king in 1648 was a bold exploration into the very nature of monarchy rather than a personal attack upon Charles himself. Secondly, the appearance of a well-disciplined citizens' army in which representative councils arose and "agitators" lectured or preached to the troops, teaching even privates (cobblers and tinkers in the satiric literature) to reflect upon political issues. Thirdly, the first effort to write and then to rewrite the constitution of a nation, thus quite literally constructing a new political order. Fourthly, the public presentation of whole sets of clamorous demands, many of them from previously passive and nonpolitical men, for the reorganization of the church, the state, the government of London, the educational system, and the administration of the poor laws. Fifthly, the formation of groups specifically and deliberately designed to implement these demands, groups based on the principle of voluntary association and requiring proof of ideological commitment but not of blood ties, aristocratic patronage, or local residence. Sixthly, the appearance of a political journalism in response to the sudden expansion of the active and interested public. Finally and above all, the sharp, insistent awareness of the need for and the possibility of *reform*. Surely one of the decisive characteristics of the new politics, this passion to remake society was clearly manifest in a sermon preached before the House of Commons in 1641:

> Reformation must be universal [exhorted the Puritan minister Thomas Case] . . . reform all places, all persons and callings; reform the benches of judgement, the inferior magistrates . . . Reform the universities, reform the cities, reform the countries, reform inferior schools of learning, reform the Sabbath, reform the ordinances, the worship of God . . . you have more work to do than I can speak . . . Every plant which my heavenly father hath not planted shall be rooted up.

The same spirit was present sixty years earlier in a group of Puritan ministers who drafted a parliamentary bill which with its first clause would have thrown down all existing "laws, customs, statutes, ordinances and constitutions" of the English church. It is hard even to conceive of a politics of such destructive sweep in the Middle Ages. It is at least equally hard to imagine the magistrates, scholars, or soldiers who would happily have set about providing new laws, customs, statutes, ordinances, and so on. In his own fashion, however, Cromwell was such a man; John Milton, who served him, was surely another. Not only the church, but the state, the household, the school, even the theater and the sports arena—religion, culture, family, and politics—all these the great Puritan poet would have made anew.

The very word *reform* took on a new meaning in the course of the sixteenth and seventeenth centuries: it had once suggested renewal, restoration to some original form or state. This was the connotation it probably carried for early Protestants with their vision of the primitive church and for many French and English lawyers who conceived and glorified an "ancient constitution." But the changes proposed in the name of these two myths were often so radical and represented, despite the appeal to custom and precedent, such a sharp departure from current practice, that reform came eventually to mean simply improvement, change for the better, indeed, radical change for the better. By the 1640's the word implied transformations of the sort associated today with revolution. That was the sense it already had for the conservative Hooker who saw reform as an endless process: "There hath arisen a sect in England which . . . seeketh to reform even the French [that is, the Huguenot] reformation." It had a similar meaning in Milton's work: "God is decreeing some new and great period in his church, even to the reforming of reformation itself." Preachers and lawyers continued, of course, to appeal to primitive and ancient practices, but the shift in meaning is clearly visible in the gradual replacement of the cyclical view of history that underlay the idea of renewal with a progressive view that provided a theoretical foundation for the idea of improvement.

The development of a theory of progress is only another sign of the new political spirit, the new sense of activity and its possibilities, the more radical imagination that mark the sixteenth and seventeenth centuries. The origins and nature of this new spirit are suggested by the fact that progress was first imagined in terms of a Christian history and an imminent millennium, or again, by the fact that it was a minister who preached so energetically of reform to the gentlemen, lawyers, and merchants of the English Commons. The Puritan cleric insisted that political activity was a creative endeavor in which the saints were privileged as well as obliged to participate. The saints were responsible for their world—as medieval men were not—and responsible above all for its continual reformation. Their enthusiastic and purposive activity was part of their religious life, not something distinct and separate: they acted out their saintliness in debates, elections, administration, and warfare. Only some sensitivity to religious zeal can make the behavior of the English in the sixteen-forties and fifties explicable. Politics for the moment was the pursuit of a religious goal; its end was joy—if only spiritual joy—as Milton surely knew and the most somber and dutiful of the saints must dimly have sensed.

But Puritan zeal was not a private passion; it was instead a highly collective emotion and it imposed upon the saints a new and impersonal discipline. Conscience freed the saints from medieval passivity and feudal loyalty, but it did not encourage the individualist, Italianate politics of faction and intrigue. Puritan ministers campaigned against the personal extravagance of the great Renaissance courtiers and deplored the role of "private interest" in politics. The conscientious activity that they favored is perhaps best revealed in Cromwell's New Model Army, with its rigid discipline, its elaborate rules against every imaginable sin from looting and rapine to blasphemy and card-playing and finally its workmanlike and efficient military tactics. Such a discipline, emphasizing self-control (or mutual surveillance), sustained commitment and systematic activity might well have its parallel in politics. Indeed, the new spirit of the Puritans can be defined as a kind of military and political work-ethic, directly analogous to the "worldly asceticism" which Max Weber has described in economic life, but oriented not toward acquisition so much as toward contention, struggle, destruction, and rebuilding. Calvinist conscience gave to war and to politics (and if Weber is right to business as well) a new sense of method and purpose. It is this above all that distinguishes the activity of the saints from that of medieval men, caught up in the unchanging world of tradition, fixed in their social place and loyal to their relatives; and also from that of Renaissance men, pursuing a purely personal ambition. . . .

The two social groups in England whose members were most likely to adopt the Calvinist ideology, to become saints, and to shape sainthood to their own needs, were the clergy and the new class of educated laymen. Professional intellectuals play a vital part in the modernization process everywhere and they are usually seconded by those amateurs of knowledge who arise out of the economic and social transformations of the traditional order, usually as leaders of the new middle classes. The role of the minister in sixteenth- and seventeenth-century England provides the occasion for an analysis of the radical intellectual as the man who first freed himself from the controls of a corporate church and who proved (perhaps because of this freedom) most sensitive to the strains of social change, most open to conversion, and most ready to experiment with underground organization and radical ideology. The sociology and politics of the Puritan clergy are examined in Chapter Four; their new ideas, the day-to-day articulation of their discontent and new-found godliness in sermons, diaries, and theological tracts, are studied in Chapters Five and Six. The highly regulated life of the ministers, the modes of their organization, the very tone of their literature, all suggest, it will be argued, a new world of discipline and work in which medieval hierarchy and patriarchy, organismic feeling, and corporate association are left far behind.

The lay saints, most often or most importantly pious gentlemen like Oliver Cromwell or university-educated merchants and lawyers who aspire to gentility, are described in Chapter Seven. Puritanism proved admirably adapted to the needs of these men—just as radicalism in different forms has often since proven itself functional to the "rise" of new social classes, or at any rate of the educated members of such classes. The annoying word "rise" which seems to denote some collective and impersonal ascent actually conceals a vast amount of painful human endeavor requiring willfulness, calculation, nerve, and perhaps above all an anxious, introspective discipline and self-control—requiring, that is, a conscience such as Calvinism supplied to its saints. At the same time, the acceptance of the new ideology by gentlemen and merchants made radical politics possible. Without the power and prerogatives of gentility, Calvinist zeal would have remained a private matter, giving rise at best to a helter-skelter rebelliousness like that of the medieval and Reformation sects or to a furtive and futile conspiracy of heretical prophets. (The English sectarians, it should be said, will not be discussed in the pages that follow; interesting as they are, they are not the crucial innovators in English political history.)

The reception of Calvinist ideas in the social milieu that produced Hampden, Pym, and Cromwell made practically possible the two forms of the new politics which followed historically upon the secret organizations of the intellectuals: godly magistracy and religious soldiery. The culmination of the two was revolution—manifest in the usurpations of Puritan parliamentarians and the "providential" victories of the New Model army. Underlying both was not only the ambition of a class but also the Calvinist conscience, with its extraordinary view of politics as work and of work as a permanent effort and an endless struggle with the devil. In the course of this struggle the discipline of an army at war and the nerves of a soldier on guard became elementary necessities of political men: the new conception of politics as a kind of war, which underlies the view the saints themselves took of the revolution, is described in Chapter Eight. Perhaps the character of these political soldiers was best revealed in the reiterated theme of a sermon preached by John Arrowsmith to the House of Commons in January of 1643, when the war was already begun. "I am confident," Arrowsmith declared, "you never dreamt of reforming a church and state with ease." If indeed men did not dream of a peaceful change, if they had been brought somehow to view violence and systematic warfare as the necessary price of reformation, this was because of the training that Calvinism provided. The traditional mentality, for which such a struggle might well have been inconceivable, was slowly worn away and finally altogether replaced by the collective and modernist conscience of the saints. . . .

Calvinism was not a liberal ideology, even though congregational life was surely a training for self-government and democratic participation. The radically democratic Levellers probably had their beginning in the Puritan congregations, in the debates, for example, that preceded the elections of ministers and in the recriminations that so frequently followed. Even when the choice of ministers was not open to the church membership, as it often was not, politics in the congregation was very different from the influence, intrigue, and patronage that prevailed at the bishop's or the king's court. Personal loyalty and deference, so highly developed among the courtiers, declined among the brethren. Calvinist voluntarism established instead the freely negotiated contract as the highest human bond; in its terms, Puritan writers described the connection of man and God, of the saint and his associates, of minister and church, of husband and wife. All these relations were entered into willingly and knowingly, and if men were thus to negotiate contracts they obviously required some knowledge of the contract's content and purposes. The preaching and writing of the ministers was designed to provide such knowledge; so was the discussion among lay Puritans of the sermons and the texts; so also the congregational debates, the reading, note-taking and diary-keeping of the newly political, newly educated saints. And all this was preparation also for the debates and elections, the pamphlets and parties of liberal politics.

But Puritanism was much more than this, as the previous description of the "attack upon the traditional world" and the "new world of discipline and work" ought to have made clear. The associations of the brethren were voluntary indeed, but they gave rise to a collectivist discipline marked above all by a tense mutual "watchfulness." Puritan individualism never led to a respect for privacy. Tender conscience had its rights, but it was protected only against the interference of worldlings and not against "brotherly admonition." And the admonitions of the brethren were anxious, insistent, continuous. They felt themselves to be living in an age of chaos and crime and sought to train conscience to be permanently on guard, permanently at war, against sin. Debate in a Puritan congregation was never a free and easy exchange of ideas; the need for vigilance, the pressures of war were too great to allow for friendly disagreement. What lay behind the warfare of the saints? Two things above all: a fierce antagonism to the traditional world and the prevailing pattern of human relation and a keen and perhaps not unrealistic anxiety about human wickedness and the dangers of social disorder. The saints attempted to fasten upon the necks of all mankind the yoke of a new political discipline—impersonal and ideological, not founded upon loyalty or affection, no more open to spontaneity than to chaos and crime. This discipline was not to depend upon the authority of paternal kings and lords or upon the obedience of childlike and trustful subjects. Puritans sought to make it voluntary, like the contract itself, the object of individual and collective willfulness. But voluntary or not, its keynote was repression.

Liberalism also required such voluntary subjection and self-control, but in sharp contrast to Puritanism, its politics was shaped by an extraordinary confidence in the possibility of both, a firm sense of human reasonableness and of the relative ease with which order might be attained. Liberal confidence made repression and the endless struggle against sin unnecessary; it also tended to make self-control invisible, that is, to forget its painful history and naïvely assume its existence. The result was that liberalism did not create the self-control it required. The Lockeian state was not a disciplinary institution as was the Calvinist holy commonwealth, but rather rested on the assumed political virtue of its citizens. It is one of the central arguments of this conclusion that Puritan repression has its place in the practical history of that strange assumption.

It is not possible to judge in any absolute terms the effectiveness of this repression or the extent of the social need for it. It can only be said that the Puritans *knew about* human sinfulness and that Locke did not need to know. This undoubtedly reflects not only different temperaments but also different experiences. The very existence and spread of Puritanism in the years before the revolution surely suggest the presence in English society of an acute fear of disorder and "wickedness"—a fear, it has been argued above, attendant upon the transformation of the old political and social order. The triumph of Lockeian ideas, on the other hand, suggests the overcoming of anxiety, the appearance of saints and citizens for whom sin is no longer a problem. The struggle against the old order seems largely to have been won by Locke's time, and the excitement, confusion, and fearfulness of that struggle almost forgotten. Lockeian liberals found it possible to dispense with religious, even with ideological, controls in human society and thought enthusiasm and battle-readiness unattractive. But this was only because the controls had already been implanted *in men*. In a sense, then, liberalism was dependent upon the existence of "saints," that is, of persons whose good behavior could be relied upon. At the same time, the secular and genteel character of liberalism was determined by the fact that these were "saints" whose goodness (socialibity, moral decency, or mere respectability) was self-assured and relaxed, free from the nervousness and fanaticism of Calvinist godliness. . . .

The significance of Puritanism lies in the part it played between 1530 and 1660. Those were crucial years of struggle and change in England and those were the years when Calvinism was a forceful, dynamic faith. After the Restoration, its energy was drawn inward, its political aspiration forgotten; the saint gave way to the nonconformist. Or, Lockeian liberalism provided an alternative political outlook. But Puritanism cannot be explained by reference either to its survivals or its transformations; it is necessary to confront the historical reality of those years when it was still an integral creed. In those years, Puritanism provided what may best be called an *ideology of transition*. It was functional to the process of modernization not because it served the purposes of some universal progress, but because it met the human needs that arise whenever traditional controls give way and hierarchical status and corporate privilege are called into question. These needs can be met in other ways: by ideologists of nostalgia, for example, who glorify the old security and the old bondage. But they are met most effectively by doctrines like Puritanism that encourage a vigorous self-control and a narrowing of energies, a bold effort to shape a new personality against the background of social "unsettledness." Once such a personality has been achieved, the saints proceed to shape society in the image of their own salvation; they become what the ideologists of nostalgia can never become: active enemies of the old order. Thus when country gentlemen have experienced a conversion like Cromwell's, they are transformed not only into saints but also into parliamentary intransigents, attacking the traditional hierarchy root and branch and experimenting with new forms of political association.

But though they appear in history as revolutionaries, who destroy the old order and kill the king, the primary source of the saints' radical character lies in their response to the *dis*order of the transition period. The old order is only a part, and not the most important part of their experience. They live much of their lives amidst the breakdown of that order or (as with the clerical intellectuals) in hiding or exile from it. Much as they hated bishops and courtiers, then, the Puritan saints hated and feared vagabonds more and dreaded the consequences of the vagabonds in themselves, their own "unsettledness." "Masterless men" are always the first products of the breakdown of tradition and the saints hardly thought such men less dangerous than did their former masters. Without the experience of masterlessness, the Puritans are unimaginable. Sainthood is one of the likely results of that experience, or rather one of the ways in which men seek to cope with that experience. Hobbist authoritarianism is another way—and the contrast between Hobbes' appeal to sovereign power and the Puritan's struggle for self-control suggests the difficulty of describing sainthood, in Erich Fromm's terms, as an "escape from freedom."

Fromm is certainly right, however, in viewing the saint in the context of "freedom." The Puritans were in no sense the products of a new order slowly growing up within traditional feudal society, as Marxist theory would have it. They were the products—though that word hardly suggests their extraordinary activism—of disorder. They inherited the critical and destructive work of writers like Machiavelli and Luther and they continued that work only after they had organized themselves to survive in the midst of criticism and destruction. They were second-generation men: they arrived in a world where courageous heretics and philosophers had already challenged the traditional masters; they encountered the difficulties of this world by being born again, by rejecting masterlessness and finding a new master in themselves and a new system of control in their godly brethren.

Coping with disorder meant being reborn as a new man, self-confident and free of worry, capable of vigorous, willful activity. The saints sometimes took new names, or gave new names to their children, to signify this rebirth. If the experience of "unsettledness" had made them anxious, depressed, unable to work, given to fantasies of demons, morbid introspection, or fearful daydreams such as Calvin had suggested were common among fallen men, then sainthood was indeed a triumph of character formation. Here the analogy with the Bolsheviks is worth pursuing. Lenin's diatribes against "slovenliness . . . carelessness, untidiness, unpunctuality, nervous haste, the inclination to substitute discussion for action, talk for work, the inclination to undertake everything under the sun without finishing anything" were intended first of all as attacks upon his fellow radicals and exiles—whatever their value as descriptions of the "primitive" Russia he hated so much. The first triumph of Bolshevism, as of Puritanism, was over the impulse toward "disorganization" in its own midst: here, so to speak, was Satan at work where he is ever most active—in the ranks of the godly. It should not be forgotten, however, that this was a triumph also over the impulse toward free thought and spontaneous expression that manifests itself with especial vigor in the period of masterlessness and with which modernity has, up to a point, made its peace. This was the sacrifice which the saints found necessary in their terrible struggle for self-control. The Puritans vigorously attacked Renaissance experimentation in dress and in all the arts of self-decoration and hated the free-wheeling vagabonds who roamed the countryside and crowded into cities, never organizing themselves into families and congregations. They dreaded the dance and the drama, tore down maypoles and closed playhouses; they waged a long, bitter and unending war against fornication. In a similar fashion, the Jacobin leader Robespierre attacked the hedonism and censured the morals of the new bourgeoisie and spitefully connected the radical free thought of the Enlightenment with anti-revolutionary conspiracy. Atheism, he declared, is aristocratic. And again Lenin, preaching with all the energy of a secular Calvinist against free love: "Dissoluteness in sexual life is bourgeois, [it] is a phenomenon of decay. The proletariat is a rising class . . . It needs clarity, clarity and again clarity. And so, I repeat, no weakening, no waste, no destruction of forces."

In fact, Lenin's morality had little to do with the proletariat and the "dissoluteness" he attacked had little to do with the bourgeoisie. He might as well have talked of saints and worldlings as the Puritans did. The contrast he was getting at was between those men who had succumbed to (or taken advantage of!) the disorder of their time—speculators in philosophy, vagabonds in their sexual lives, economic Don Juans—and those who had somehow pulled themselves out of "unsettledness," organized their lives and regained control. The first group were the damned and the second the saved. The primary difference between them was not social, but ideological.

All forms of radical politics make their appearance at moments of rapid and decisive change, moments when customary status is in doubt and character (or "identity") is itself a problem. Before Puritans, Jacobins, or Bolsheviks attempt the creation of a new order, they must create new men. Repression and collective discipline are the typical methods of this creativity: the disordered world is interpreted as a world at war; enemies are discovered and attacked. The saint is a soldier whose battles are fought out in the self before they are fought out in society. Revolution follows from Puritan sainthood—that is, from the triumph over Satanic lusts—and also from Jacobin virtue and from the Bolshevik "steeling" of character; it is the acting out of a new identity, painfully won. This connection between sainthood and revolution is nicely illustrated in John Milton's eulogy of Cromwell: "A commander first over himself; the conqueror of himself, it was over himself he had learnt most to triumph. Hence he went to encounter with an external enemy as a veteran accomplished in all military duties . . ." In traditional societies, this self-conquest is not necessary—except for relatively small numbers of men who for personal reasons choose monasticism as a way of life. In modern societies, it is routine. But there is a point in the modernization process when large numbers of men, suddenly masterless, seek a rigid self-control; when they discover new purposes, dream of a new order, organize their lives for disciplined and methodical activity. These men are prospective saints and citizens; for them Puritanism, Jacobinism, and Bolshevism are appropriate options. At this point in time, they are likely options.

This is not to reduce political radicalism to the psychological therapy of "unsettled" men. The "unsettledness" which Knox, Cartwright, and Cromwell experienced, with all its attendant fearfulness and enthusiasm, sometimes disfiguring and sometimes ennobling, was only a heightened form of the feelings of many of their fellow Englishmen—for ultimately the sociological range of the Puritan response was very wide. Of course, "unsettledness" was not a permanent condition and so sainthood was only a temporary role. The Puritans failed in their effort to transform England into a holy commonwealth and, in one way or another, their more recent counterparts have also failed. Sainthood mediated the dangerous shift from one social routine to another; then it survived only as a remembered enthusiasm and a habitual self-control devoid, as Weber's capitalism is, of theological reason. What this suggests, however, is not that holiness was an impractical dream, the program of neurotic, muddled, or unrealistic men. In fact, Puritan ministers and elders (and fathers) had considerable political experience and the holy commonwealth was in part achieved—among those men who most needed holiness. Nor is it correct to argue from the inability of the saints to retain political power that Puritanism represented only a temporary triumph of "ideas" over "interests," of the holiness doctrine over the ultimately more significant secular purposes of gentlemen, merchants, and lawyers. For what needs to be explained is precisely why the saints over a long period of time acquired such an intense interest in ideas like predestination and holiness. Puritan ideology was a response to real experience, therefore a practical effort to cope with personal and social problems. The disappearance of the militant saints from English politics in the years after the Restoration suggests only that these problems were limited in time to the period of breakdown and psychic and political reconstruction. When men stopped being afraid or became less afraid, then Puritanism was suddenly irrelevant. Particular elements of the Puritan system were transformed to fit the new routine—and other elements were forgotten. And only then did the saint become a man of "good behavior," cautious, respectable, moved only by a routine anxiety and ready to participate in a Lockeian society.

IV. SUMMARY

John T. McNeill

CALVIN'S IDEAS STILL POLITICALLY RELEVANT TODAY

NO responsible Christian can be without concern for civil government. This follows not only from the fact that governments are obliged to take measures affecting the Christian community, but also from ethical principles inherent in original and historic Christianity. Even those Christian groups whose members are required to abstain from political activity affirm theories of the state by which such abstention is justified. Political indifference on the part of Christians is not a mark of superior piety but of defective ethics.

It is true that in our environment, where church and state have minimal intercourse, a minister may choose to keep silent on public issues without greatly exposing himself to reproach for neglect of his proper obligations. Such an option was hardly open to a Christian leader in Calvin's world, where the impact of political acts and policies on the course of church reform was constant, powerful, and inescapable. Detachment from these political stresses was unthinkable for John Calvin, the son of a law clerk, a graduate in law, a classicist familiar with the political treatises of Plato and Aristotle, Cicero and Seneca, and a man intent on reforms that were to shake the thrones of the mighty. His concentration on Biblical studies and his labor and care for the church did not eradicate his political interest but gave to it a new dimension; the magistrate became, for man's earthly order of life, a vicar of God. It need not surprise us to find that from his Commentary on Seneca's *Treatise on Clemency* of 1532 until that hour in 1564 when from his deathbed he urged the magistrates of Geneva so to rule as to "preserve this republic in its present happy condition," his writings are strewn with penetrating comments on the policies of rulers and illuminating passages on the principles of government. . . .

FORMS OF GOVERNMENT

The habitual reference by Calvin to the divine basis of government gives color to the use of such terms as "theocracy," "bibliocracy," "christocracy" by some writers who describe his ideal of a political society as well as the disciplined community of Geneva under his sway. That such terms have been proposed as keys to his political intention is itself significant. But they are not free from ambiguity and are not very helpful toward an understanding of his mind or his Geneva. If "theocracy" is take in its popular sense of hierocracy, government by priests, rather than in its basic meaning, government by God, it is an inappropriate way to describe the situation at Geneva, for there Calvin separates the magistrate from the clergy. He and his ministerial associates held no political offices or magisterial authority in Geneva. If "bibliocracy" means a government based on Biblical principles, it is vaguely applicable; but not if it implies a basis of Biblical legislation. The notion that a modern state must not be "ruled by the common laws of nations" but in accordance with "the political system of Moses" Calvin explicitly rejects as "seditious, false, and foolish." The eminent visitor who saw in Calvin's Geneva "the most perfect school of Christ" might have been willing to apply the term "Christocracy" in this connection. And Calvin's statement that "kings and princes should not think it a disgrace to them to prostrate

From *Calvinism and the Political Order*, editor George L. Hunt, consulting editor John T. McNeill, pp. 23–24, 34–45. Reprinted by permission of The Westminster Press.

themselves suppliantly before Christ, the King of Kings" has many parallels in his writings. But the term is not comprehensive enough. His political thought ranges beyond Christian governments. In areas where Christ's kingship is not thought of by ruler or people he sees the civic order as a valid organ of the divine purpose functioning through natural law. André Biéler has recently written:

> The question whether the magistrates must personally be Christians is fundamentally not very important. Calvin wanted them to be so. But in his encouragements to the persecuted churches he well demonstrated that the obedience of Christians to the magistrates is by no means conditioned by the faith or by the lack of faith of these authorities.

Obedience, and the limitations of obedience, do not differ by reason of the ruler's religion; the issue arises, rather, where he commands what God forbids.

Calvin did not draw up a utopian scheme of government and he is content to be somewhat inexplicit with regard to the ideal structure of the state. In general, he views any existing government as a thing given and not to be called in question. He often ranges kings, magistrates, and other officers indifferently, as alike God-ordained and so to be revered and obeyed and as alike responsible for the public good. He was, of course, familiar with the treatment of forms of government by ancient writers and like them he was well aware that good government is not automatically assured through the adoption of any one of these. "It is not easy," he confesses, "to distinguish which one of them excels in usefulness." We are not justified in tagging him with a label that would identify him with any modern political school. To his cultured despisers on the left his stress on obedience has made him a political and social reactionary, whereas to those on the right his espousal of the freedom and welfare of the people marks him as a dangerous revolutionary. His partisans, in turn, have tended to find in his pages support for their own political preferences, or even their own political indifference. The passage in which he briefly but explicitly compares monarchy, aristocracy, and democracy reflects the commonplaces of the Greek philosophers. Each form has its typical perversions. Kingship may lapse into tyranny, aristocracy into the faction of a few, and still more readily, the rule of the people into sedition. This much Calvin and his contemporaries learned from Plato, Aristotle, and Cicero. A few years earlier Zwingli had similarly stated the matter with the declaration that "we must be alert" to prevent such deterioration. But Calvin had an afterthought that must be held to cancel his seeming indifference to forms of government. When settled in Geneva, in the 1543 edition of the *Institutes* he introduced into this paragraph a frank statement of preference:

> For if the three forms of government which the philosophers discuss be considered in themselves, I will not deny that aristocracy, or a system compounded of aristocracy and democracy (*vel aristocratian vel temperatum ex ipsa et politia statum*) far excels all others.

And what is aristocracy in Calvin's vocabulary? The whole passage shows that the words of Greek origin used in it are used in their classical sense. For Plato aristocracy is "government by the best," the rule of "the truly good and just man." For Aristotle it is "the distribution of honors according to virtue (*aréte*)," since "virtue is the defining factor of aristocracy, as wealth is of oligarchy and freedom of democracy." Once in this context Calvin uses Cicero's word "optimates" for the best men, a word which historically sometimes stood for members of the best families, but is apparently here employed in innocence of such implication. Now he does not tell us here how the excellent men become magistrates. But it may be significant that the phrase "compounded of aristocracy and democracy" was set into the *Institutes* in the year in which Calvin participated in the revision of the constitution of Geneva. By this constitution the four syndics who were the chief magistrates of the city were elected by the General Council of all citizens, but they were not nominated by it. A list of eight names was prepared by the Little Council and presented to the General Council which by vote elected four of the eight. As for the Little Council, it filled its ranks by co-optation, subject to the approval of the Council of Two Hundred, whose membership was also nominated by the Little Council. This is "aristocracy compounded with democracy," Geneva style. Essentially it existed before Calvin's time but it was retouched by him. It is an aristocracy of excellence, not of lineage, checked by the democracy of popular election. The "best men" are chosen by popular vote from a restricted list of names selected by their experienced predecessors in office.

The system illustrates a principle that Calvin was to state more explicitly by another insertion in the same section in his 1559 edition. Here he explains his preference for the aristocracy-democracy type of government on the ground that kings actually lack that self-control, discernment of justice, acumen, and prudence needed for sound government, so that "it is safer and more bearable for a number to exercise government" (*ut tutius sit ac magis tolerabile plures tenere gubernacula*) "so that they may help, teach and admonish one another; and if one asserts himself unfairly there may be a number to restrain his wilfulness." Calvin finds this model regimen in Ex., ch. 18, and Deut., ch. 1, and declares most happily that government in which "freedom is regulated with becoming moderation and is properly established on a durable basis." Where such freedom exists, magistrates are to be alert and careful to preserve it; else they are "faithless men, and traitors to their country." With this important passage may be linked his statement of the same period that kingship by hereditary right seems not to be in accord with liberty and that a well-ordered government is derived from the general vote of the people. But basically it is perhaps not the fact of hereditary succession that repels Calvin so much as the assumption that one mortal man, by his own talents and with no one to say him nay, is competent to meet the responsibilities of government. Where high decisions are made he finds safety in plurality (*plures*) and in the consequent opportunity of mutual admonition and the pooling of wisdom. And even the "best men" have to pass the test of the ballot box.

RESISTANCE TO TYRANNY

Much has been written about resistance to tyranny as a significant element of Calvin's political thought. Its significance is hardly lessened by the fact that it received scant space in his writings. For his conservative mind it was difficult to make a place for any resistance by subjects even to the most oppressive ruler. Yet the topic creeps into some of his commentaries and is given remarkable prominence in the closing paragraphs of the *Institutes*. We must submit, says Calvin, meanwhile imploring the help of God. But as Israel was delivered from the tyranny of Pharaoh through Moses and later sometimes chastised by foreign enemies who were unwittingly acting as agents of the divine will, so God by such means "breaks the bloody scepters of arrogant kings" and "overturns intolerable governments." The obvious inference is that we are to acquiesce in revolutions in which oppressive regimes are overthrown. Audaciously, Calvin adds: "*Audeant principes et terreantur*, Let princes hear and be afraid!" These words are in every edition of the *Institutes*. In the first edition they must have been consciously flung back by the young exile at King Francis I under whom Calvin's friends were being tortured and burned.

He notes, moreover, in some states the existence of "magistrates of the people (*magistratus populares*)" whose function it is to check the despotism and licentiousness of kings. Such were the ephors of Sparta, the tribunes of Rome, and the demarchs of Athens, and "perhaps," he adds with seeming casualness, "the three estates of modern realms." These magistracies are by God's ordinance protectors of the freedom of the people, and it is nefarious perfidy on their part to wink at royal oppression of the common folk. Here too, as often elsewhere, Calvin reminds his readers that there is always one reservation to be observed in connection with the obligation of political obedience; the prior requirement is obedience to God. Two years after the last Latin edition of the *Institutes,* commenting on Dan. 6:22, "Before thee, O King, I have done no hurt," he observes:

> For earthly princes lay aside their power when they rise up against God, and are unworthy to be reckoned among the number of mankind. We ought rather utterly to defy them [*conspuere in ipsorum capita,* literally, to spit on their very heads] than to obey them.

This is rough language even for a fighting theologian: its tone reveals Calvin's perturbation over the untoward events of 1561.

In seizing upon the ephors and tribunes of antiquity for his argument on the restraining power of popular magistrates, Calvin may have been indebted to Zwingli, who, however, omits the demarchs and applies the reference to the authority, not of magistrates, but of pastors. But the argument grows out of Calvin's whole structure of thought. It is consistent with his constant rejection of any right vested in the private citizen to resist his ruler. We are to wait until intolerable government is overturned either by God's use of the wrath of men or by action of the constitutional defenders of liberty. It is consistent with his attitude to the Conspiracy of Amboise, whose leader he judged, not one of those *magistratus populares* who were appointed to withstand royal oppression, but a political hothead, unauthorized and irresponsible. It is true that where no constitutional defenders of the people's liberty exist in a state Calvin gives no lead for possible resistance. But he must have known that nearly all European states had developed and were employing some organs of representation and more or less effective checks on absolutism, though in his native France the meeting of the Estates was only a memory and a hope. After his death, Calvin's more aggressive friend Francis Hotman, and more than a century later the Huguenot writer Pierre Jurieu, were among the strong advocates of the power of the Estates as over against that of the king; and the tradition reaches to the revolutionary Estates General of 1789. The "ephors" passage became a commonplace of Reformed political writing for generations. Calvin's single sentence of 88 Latin words proved more impressive, perhaps even more influential, than his countless warnings against disobedience. . .

ENDURING VALUE OF CALVIN'S POLITICAL INSIGHTS

The highly gifted Reformer of Geneva died four hundred years ago, in 1564. But he has come to life for many readers in our own generation. Has he any wisdom for civil government from which, in our vastly different conditions, we may profit today?

Obviously we are forbidden by our total political situation from imitating the church-state complex of Calvin's Geneva. His contribution to us, if any, is mainly in the realm of principles. May I attempt to list a few points where I think we may find helpful suggestions in his teachings?

1. Calvin sets the example of a positive attitude to government and a deep appreciation of the ruler's office. He holds that for the Christian the business of government is not something alien or negligible. The state is a divinely given boon for man's safety and peace, and political activity is a realm of Christian duty. For all who in any sense stand in the Calvinian tradition this is a legacy not to be cast aside. Have we not here a lesson and an example by which we may become more effective Christians? Indeed, Calvin's teaching in this field would seem worthy of attention by all our contemporaries as the testimony of a singularly perceptive mind keenly aware of the political world while primarily concerned for the church and Christian truth.

2. It is worth keeping in remembrance that for Calvin the aim of gov-

ernment is the public good, conceived in the broad sense of service to every human person in his welfare, his education, his opportunity to inherit the treasures of culture and religion. He values highly a dedicated faithfulness and honesty in public men, since in their calling they are instruments of God. We have something here far above the level of the political life to which, alas, we have become accustomed. One would not go idly junketing on public revenues if he reflected that these funds are as blood drawn from the people. Nor would the citizen and voter be swayed by inducements and promises in which he, or his area, is to be the recipient of federal aid disproportionate to need.

3. Calvin is a realist in his political expectations. He sets the standards high; but he does not expect sinless perfection in political man. Monarchy, one-man rule, is called unsatisfactory because no one man has the character and the brains for such responsibility. History is on Calvin's side here. It is replete with illustrations of the misery of rule under self-glorifying despots whether set up by hereditary right or by aggressive action. There is always danger where power accumulates in the hands of one, or of too few. Authority is best exercised by constituted bodies in which a constructive mutual criticism is maintained. Let me add that a constructive mutual criticism does not mean the art of winning elections by defamation of character.

4. To paraphrase Calvin, "Let Christians hear and be afraid." Have we not been culpably negligent of efforts to set forth and inculcate high political ideals? Have we not scolded the politicians where they have offended without showing unto them a more excellent way? It has been my privilege to hear thousands of sermons. On specific and local public issues I have often heard a true note sounded. But I am afraid that I could count on the fingers of one hand any substantial pulpit utterances calculated to direct Christian thinking along the higher ranges of political service, to impart to the citizen as voter and member of society a vital sense of his general political responsibility, and to guide Christian youth looking for a worthy vocation toward a dedicated career in politics. I hope we may say that we have begun to recover lost ground here. But I believe that there has been in this century no adequate attempt on the part of the churches to confront the nations and the world with a Christian political philosophy. The *Woodrow Wilson Lectures* have been planned I know, not merely as a means of recovering a proud tradition, but also in order to stimulate a greatly needed Christian participation in "civil government."

If in our time the realm of politics is to be redeemed from corruption and triviality and snarling partisanship, the church has a function to perform that it has too much neglected. It will not be a waste of time to sit for a while at Calvin's feet.

SUGGESTIONS FOR ADDITIONAL READING

IN the spring of 1564, as he lay dying, John Calvin called the ministers of Geneva to his side to review his labors in that city. Among other things, he noted that he was but "a poor timid scholar" who had tried to do the work of God "amidst extraordinary struggles." His dying memories were not happy ones, and he seemed to look forward to the tranquility of death. However, the grave did not put an end to the controversy which had so marked his life and work at Geneva. The "poor timid scholar" has been the object of thousands of studies on a multitude of subjects from the hour he breathed his last until the present. And there is no sign of any lessening of interest in Calvin and his influence on the Western World. To the contrary, even in the twentieth century he continues to be one of the most written about men in history.

Obviously, the following list of suggested readings is highly selective. However, preference has been given to those older works which have been most widely accepted among scholars and to the most promising newer studies. Those items marked by an asterisk are represented by extracts earlier in this volume.

JOURNALS, BIBLIOGRAPHIES AND GENERAL HISTORIES

A number of scholarly journals often feature essays of interest to students of Calvin and Calvinism: the *Archiv für Reformationsgeschichte*, a bilingual periodical devoted to Reformation studies, hereafter cited as *ARG; Church History*, a publication of the American Society of Church History, hereafter *CH;* the *Journal of Ecclesiastical History*, sponsored by a group of English church historians; the *Bibliothèque d'Humanisme et Renaissance*, published in Geneva with articles in several languages; the *Bulletin de la Société de l'histoire due protestantisme français*, official journal of the French Protestant Historical Society, hereafter *BSHPF;* the *Revue d'histoire ecclésiastique*, published by the University of Louvain, Belgium, hereafter *RHE;* and the *American Historical Review* of the American Historical Association, hereafter *AHR*.

Several key bibliographies attempt systematically to list the vast and almost unmanageable body of Calvin literature. Alfred Erichson's *Bibliographia Calviniana* (Nieuwkoop, 1960) was first published in 1900 and recently has been reissued. Wilhelm Niesel's *Calvin Bibliographie, 1901–1959* (Munich, 1961) brings Erichson up to 1959. Also helpful are the annotated bibliographies of John T. McNeill, "Thirty Years of Calvin Study," *CH*, XVII (1948), and Edward A. Dowey, Jr., "Studies in Calvin and Calvinism Since 1948," *CH*, XXIV (1955) and "Studies in Calvin and Calvinism Since 1955," *CH*, XXIX (1960). Three other bibliographies of interest to students of Calvinism and democracy worth mentioning are Henri Hauser, *Les Sources de l'histoire de France. Le XVIe siècle (1494–1610)*, 4 vols. (Paris 1906–1915); Felix Gilbert, "Political Thought of the Renaissance and Reformation: A Report on Recent Scholarship," *Huntington Library Quarterly*, IV (1941); and J. L. Garrett, "Studies of the Sixteenth-Century Protestant Reformation: The Literature in English, 1946–1966," *The Review and Expositor*, LXIV (1967).

The most comprehensive of a number of good histories of the Reformation is Harold J. Grimm's *The Reformation Era*, rev. ed. (New York, 1965). Eminently readable are Roland Bainton, *The Reformation of the Sixteenth Century* (Boston, 1952); E. Harris Harbison, *The Age of the Reformation* (Ithaca, 1955); and G. R. Elton, *Reformation Europe, 1517–1559* (London, 1963). Also of value in understanding the place of

Calvinism in the history of the sixteenth century are H. G. Koenigsberger and George L. Mosse, *Europe in the Sixteenth Century* (New York, 1968) and Emile G. Léonard, *Histoire générale du Protestantisme,* 3 vols. (Paris, 1961–1965). Volume I of Léonard's work has been translated into English as *The Reformation* (London, 1965).

There is no standard history of Reformation political ideas. However, J. H. Hallowell's *Main Currents in Modern Political Thought* (New York, 1950) is a good place to start because he is unusually aware of the theological presuppositions upon which most modern political theory is based. Also worth consulting are R. W. and A. J. Carlyle, *A History of Mediaeval Political Theory in the West,* 6 vols. (Edinburgh, 1903–1936), vol. VI: *Political Theory from 1300 to 1600* is very good; J. N. Figgis, *Political Thought from Gerson to Grotius: 1414–1625* (Cambridge, 1907); R. H. Murray, *Political Consequences of the Reformation* (London, 1926); J. W. Allen, *A History of Political Thought in the Sixteenth Century* (London, 1929); Pierre Mesnard, *L'essor de la philosophie politique au XVIe siècle en France* (Paris, 1936); and Perez Zagorin, *A History of Political Thought in the English Revolution* (London, 1954).

A number of scholars have explored the overall influence of Calvin and Calvinism upon Western politics and culture. Among the older classics are Georg Jellinek, *Die Erklärung der Menschen und Bürgerrechte* (Leipzig, 1895); R. H. Tawney, *Religion and the Rise of Capitalism* (New York, 1926); Max Weber, *The Protestant Ethic and the Spirit of Capitalism* (New York, 1930); and Ernst Troeltsch, *The Social Teaching of the Christian Churches,* 2 vols. (London, 1931). John T. McNeill's *The History and Character of Calvinism,* rev. ed. (New York, 1967) is the best single volume on that subject but can be supplemented with profit by an older work by B. B. Warfield, *Calvin and Calvinism* (New York, 1931). G. H. Dodge has traced *The Political Theory of the Huguenots of the Dispersion* (New York, 1947). Finally, G. L. Hunt has edited a collection of stimulating essays which deal with various Calvinist political thinkers from Calvin himself to Woodrow Wilson: *Calvinism and the Political Order* (Philadelphia, 1965).

CALVIN AND GENEVA

Nearly all of Calvin's works have been published in the monumental *Calvini opera quae supersunt omnia,* 56 vols., Baum, Cunitz and Reuss, eds., in the *Corpus reformatorum,* vols. 29–87 (Brunswick, 1863–1900). Those few sermons and other fragments which escaped the *Calvini opera* are now being published as *Supplementa Calviniana,* edited by an international committee of scholars. The best critical edition of the *Institutes* in English is the *Institutes of the Christian Religion,* 2 vols., John T. McNeill ed., Ford L. Battles, trans., in the "Library of Christian Classics," XX and XXI (Philadelphia, 1960). Much of Calvin's correspondence is available in translation in *Letters of John Calvin,* 4 vols., Jules Bonnet, ed. (Philadelphia, 1858); and his *Commentaries,* 45 vols. (Edinburgh, 1843–1855) were reprinted in 1948 by Eerdman's of Grand Rapids, Michigan. A new edition and translation of Calvin's New Testament commentaries was begun in 1959 under the editorship of D. W. and T. F. Torrance. Rich in Calvin materials is the recently published *Registres de la Compagnie des Pasteurs de Genève au temps de Calvin,* 2 vols., Robert M. Kingdon and J.-F. Bergier, eds. (Geneva, 1962–1964), translated in abridged form by Philip E. Hughes as *The Registers of the Pastors of Geneva in the Time of Calvin* (Grand Rapids, 1966).

The definitive biography of Calvin remains to be written. Despite its obvious pro-Calvin leaning, Émile Doumergue's *Jean Calvin, les hommes et les choses de son temps,** 7 vols. (Lausanne, 1899–1927) remains the most detailed and informative work on Calvin yet published. Among many lesser biographies, the following are recommended: Williston Walker, *John Calvin* (New York, 1906), old but still valuable; Karl Holl, *Johannes Calvin* (Tübingen, 1928); R. N. Carew Hunt, *Calvin* (London,

1933); James Mackinnon, *Calvin and the Reformation* (London, 1936), highly critical; J. D. Benoît, *Jean Calvin* (Carrières sous Poissy, 1948); T. H. L. Parker, *Portrait of Calvin* (London, 1954), and Jean Cadier, *The Man God Mastered* (London, 1960), a sympathetic brief introduction.

The best treatments of Calvin's religious thought are by Wilhelm Niesel, *The Theology of Calvin* (London, 1956) and François Wendel, *Calvin: the Origins and Development of his Religious Thought* (New York, 1963). A great deal of light has been shed upon certain aspects of Calvin's life and thought by Quirinus Breen, *John Calvin, A Study in French Humanism* (Grand Rapids, 1932); Basil Hall, *John Calvin, Humanist and Theologian* (London, 1956); Georgia Harkness, *John Calvin; the Man and His Ethics*, rev. ed. (New York, 1958); and *John Calvin*, G. E. Duffield, ed. (Grand Rapids, 1966), vol. I of *Courtenay Studies in Reformation Theology*, a collection of essays of varying worth. Also helpful as a necessary background for understanding Calvin's political ideas are T. F. Torrance, *Calvin's Doctrine of Man* (London, 1949); Edward A. Dowey, Jr., *The Knowledge of God in Calvin's Theology* (New York, 1952); T. H. L. Parker, *The Doctrine of the Knowledge of God· A Study in the Theology of John Calvin* (Edinburgh, 1952); R. S. Wallace, *Calvin's Doctrine of the Christian Life* (Edinburgh, 1959); and two works by André Biéler, *La Pensée économique et sociale de Calvin* (Geneva, 1959) and *The Social Humanism of Calvin*, trans. by P. T. Fuhrmann (Richmond, 1964).

Several works which reveal what Geneva was like, before, during and after Calvin's years there, include Amédée Roget, *Histoire du peuple de Genève depuis la Réforme jusqu'à l'Escalade*, 7 vols. (Geneva, 1870–1883), extremely valuable; *Histoire de Genève des origines à 1798*, published by the Société D'Histoire et D'Archéologie de Genève (Geneva, 1951), rich footnotes and bibliography; and two recent volumes by E. W. Monter, *Studies in Genevan Government, 1536–1605* (Geneva, 1964) and *Calvin's Geneva* (New York, 1967).

The following books and articles represent the major contributions in the twentieth century to the continuing controversy over the question of Calvin's role in the development of modern democracy: Francis de Crue, *L'Action politique de Calvin hors de Genève* (Geneva, 1909); Gisbert Beyerhaus, *Studien zur Staatsanschauung Calvins* (Berlin, 1910); Hans Baron, *Calvins Staatsanschauung und das konfessionelle Zeitalter* (Berlin, 1924) and "Calvinist Republicanism and its Historical Roots," * *CH*, VIII (1939); Georges de Lagarde, *Recherches sur l'esprit politique de la Réforme** (Paris, 1926); H. D. Foster, "Calvin's Plan for a Puritan State in Geneva," in *Collected Papers of Herbert Darling Foster* (New York, 1929); R. N. Carew Hunt, "Calvin's Theory of the State," *Church Quarterly Review*, CVIII (1929); Charles Mercier, "L'esprit de Calvin et la démocratie," * *RHE*, XXX (1934); Josef Bohatec, *Calvin und das Recht* (Feudingen, 1934) and *Calvins Lehre von Staat und Kirche** (Breslau, 1937); V. H. Rutgers, "Le Calvinisme et l'état chrétien," *BSHPF*, LXXXIV (1935); M.-E. Chenevière, *La pensée politique de Calvin* * (Geneva, 1937); Winthrop S. Hudson, "Democratic Freedom and Religious Faith in the Reformed Tradition," * *CH*, XV (1946); John T. McNeill, "The Democratic Element in Calvin's Thought," * *CH*, XVIII (1949) and "John Calvin on Civil Government," * in *Calvinism and the Political Order*, G. L. Hunt, ed. (Philadelphia, 1965); also McNeill has edited *Calvin On God and Political Duty* (New York, 1956), excerpts from Calvin's *Institutes* with a useful introduction by the editor; and W. A. Mueller, *Church and State in Luther and Calvin* (Nashville, 1954).

CONTINENTAL CALVINISM

Histories of the spread of Calvinism to various parts of Europe include H. M. Baird, *History of the Rise of the Huguenots of France*, 2 vols. (New York, 1896); Herman de Vries de Heekelingen, *Genève pépinière du calvinisme holland-*

ais, 2 vols. (The Hague, 1924); Imre Revesz, *History of the Hungarian Reformed Church* (New York, 1956); and Samuel Mours, *Le protestantisme en France au seizième siècle* (Paris, 1959).

There is no definitive history of the French Reformation or the Wars of Religion. Various facets of the period are discussed by Henri Hauser, "The French Reformation and the French People in the Sixteenth Century," *AHR,* IV (1898); Edward Armstrong, *The French Wars of Religion* (Oxford, 1904); J.-H. Mariéjol, *La Réforme et la Ligue* in Ernest Lavisse, *Histoire de France,* vol. VI (Paris, 1904); Pierre Imbart de la Tour, *Les origines de la Réforme,* 4 vols. (Paris, 1905–1935); J. W. Thompson, *The Wars of Religion in France, 1559–1576* (Chicago, 1909); Lucien Romier, *Les origines politiques des guerres de religion,* 2 vols. (Paris, 1913–1914) and *Le royaume de Catherine de Médicis,* 2 vols. (Paris, 1925); Henri Naef, *La Conjuration d'Amboise et Genève* (Geneva, 1922); Maurice Wilkinson, *A History of the League or Sainte Union, 1576–1595* (Glasgow, 1929); J. E. Neale, *The Age of Catherine de Medici* (London, 1943); Robert M. Kingdon, *Geneva and the Coming of the Wars of Religion in France, 1555–1563* (Geneva, 1956) and *Geneva and the Consolidation of the French Protestant Movement, 1564–1572* (Madison, 1967); Vittorio de Caprariis, *Propaganda e pensiero politico in Francia durante le guerre di religione* (Naples, 1959); Philippe Erlanger, *The Massacre of Saint Bartholomew* (New York, 1962); Henri Noguères, *The Massacre of Saint Bartholomew* (New York, 1962); Julien Coudy, *Les Guerres de Religion* (Paris, 1962); Natalie Zemon Davis, "Strikes and Salvation at Lyons," *ARG,* LVI (1965); and Robert M. Kingdon, "Problems of Religious Choice for Sixteenth-Century Frenchmen," *Journal of Religious History,* IV (1966). The booklet in this series edited by J. H. M. Salmon, *The French Wars of Religion* (Boston, 1967) should be consulted for further reading.

For information on sixteenth-century French political institutions, see Roger Doucet, *Les institutions de la France au XVI*ᵉ *siècle,* 2 vols. (Paris, 1948) and Gaston Zeller's one-volume work of the same title (Paris, 1948).

The role of the Calvinists in the Dutch Revolution is examined in Pieter Geyl, *The Revolt of the Netherlands, 1555–1609* (London, 1932) and Charles Mercier, "Les théories politiques des calvinistes dans les Pays-Bas à la fin du XVIᵉ début du XVIIᵉ siècle," *RHE,* XXIX (1933).

Several biographies and studies of the political thought of certain men of the period which shed light on the subject at hand are A. W. Whitehead, *Gaspard de Coligny* (London, 1904); *Guillaume Farel, 1489–1565,* a biography and collection of documents published by a committee of Farel scholars (Paris, 1930); Raoul Patry, *Philippe du Plessis-Mornay, un Huguenot homme d'état, 1549–1623* (Paris, 1933); Philippe Erlanger, *Henri III* (Paris, 1948); Paul-F. Geisendorf, *Théodore de Bèze* (Geneva, 1949); Robert D. Linder, *The Political Ideas of Pierre Viret* (Geneva, 1964); N. M. Sutherland, *Catherine de Medici and the Ancien Régime* (London, 1966); and Nancy L. Roelker, *Queen of Navarre: Jeanne d'Albret, 1528–1572* (Cambridge, Mass., 1968).

The following monographs on various aspects of Calvinist political theory and practice in the sixteenth century are helpful: Alfred Cartier, "Les idées politiques de Théodore de Bèze," *Bulletin, Société d'histoire et d'archéologie de Genève,* II (1900); F. C. Palm, *Politics and Religion in Sixteenth-Century France* (Boston, 1927); Henri Strohl, "Le droit à la résistance d'après les conceptions protestantes," *Revue d'histoire et de philosophie religieuses,* X (1930); Beatrice Reynolds, *Proponents of Limited Monarchy in Sixteenth-Century France: Francis Hotman and Jean Bodin* (New York, 1931); Charles Mercier, "Les théories politiques des calvinistes en France au cours des guerres de religion," *BSHPF,* LXXXIII (1934); W. F. Church, *Constitutional Thought in Sixteenth-Century France* (Cambridge, Mass., 1941); R. E. Davies, *The Problem of Authority in the Continental*

Reformers (London, 1946); H. G. Koenigsberger, "The Organization of Revolutionary Parties in France and the Netherlands during the Sixteenth Century," * *Journal of Modern History*, XXVII (1955); four essays by Robert M. Kingdon, "The First Expression of Theodore Beza's Political Ideas," *ARG*, XLVI (1955), "The Political Resistance of the Calvinists in France and the Low Countries," *CH*, XXVII (1958), "Genève et les réformés français: le cas d'Hugues Sureau, dit du Rosier (1565–1574)," *Bulletin, Société d'histoire et d'archéologies de Genève*, XII (1962), and "Calvinism and Democracy: some political implications of debates on French Reformed Church government, 1562–1572," * *AHR*, LXIX (1964); and Robert D. Linder, "Pierre Viret and the Sixteenth-Century French Protestant Revolutionary Tradition," *Journal of Modern History*, XXXVIII (1966).

CALVINISM IN ENGLAND AND SCOTLAND

For general accounts of the Reformation in England, see Philip Hughes, *The Reformation in England*, 3 vols. (London, 1950–1954), a Roman Catholic view; G. R. Elton, *England under the Tudors* (London, 1955), interpretative but well-written; and A. G. Dickens, *The English Reformation* (New York, 1964), scholarly and judicious.

Connections between continental and English Calvinism have been studied by C. D. Cremeans, *The Reception of Calvinist Thought in England* (Urbana, 1949); J. H. M. Salmon, *The French Religious Wars in English Political Thought* (Oxford, 1949); and Robert D. Linder, "Pierre Viret and the Sixteenth-Century English Protestants," *ARG*, LVIII (1967).

There are a number of sound works on the origins and history of early English Puritanism including William Haller, *The Rise of Puritanism* (New York, 1938); M. M. Knappen, *Tudor Puritanism* (Chicago, 1939); Leonard J. Trinterud, "The Origins of Puritanism," *CH*, XX (1951); and a stimulating new book by Patrick Collinson, *The Elizabethan Puritan Movement* (London, 1967).

The nature of Puritan political ideas is dealt with in H. D. Foster, "The Political Theories of Calvinists before the Puritan Exodus to America," * *AHR*, XXI (1916); A. F. S. Pearson, *Church and State: Political Aspects of Sixteenth-Century Puritanism* (Cambridge, 1928); George L. Mosse, *The Holy Pretense: A Study in Christianity and Reason of State from William Perkins to John Winthrop* (Oxford, 1957); and Christopher Hill, *Society and Puritanism in Pre-Revolutionary England* (London, 1964), a Marxist approach. A closely related matter, the influence of the Puritans on English political thought and practice, is handled by J. S. Flynn, *The Influence of Puritanism in the Political and Religious Thought of the English* (London, 1920); George L. Mosse, *The Struggle for Sovereignty in England: From the Reign of Queen Elizabeth to the Petition of Right* (East Lansing, 1950); E. M. Howse, *Saints in Politics: The Clapham Sect and the Growth of Freedom* (Toronto, 1952); Christopher Morris, *Political Thought in England; Tyndale to Hooker* (London, 1953); and Leo F. Solt, "Revolutionary Calvinist Parties in England Under Elizabeth I and Charles I," *CH*, XXVII (1958).

For information on the English Civil War, see C. V. Wedgwood, *The King's Peace, 1637–1641* (London, 1955) and *The King's War 1641–1647* (London, 1958); and Ivan Root, *The Great Rebellion* (London, 1966). Among the many studies concerning the Puritans and the Civil War, the following are particularly helpful: A. S. P. Woodhouse, *Puritanism and Liberty, Being the Army Debates, 1647–1649*, 2nd ed. (Chicago, 1951); William Haller, *Liberty and Reformation in the Puritan Revolution* (New York, 1955); Geoffrey F. Nuttall, *Visible Saints: The Congregational Way, 1640–1660* (Oxford, 1957); George Yule, *The Independents in the English Civil War* (Cambridge, 1958); S. A. Burrell, "The Covenant Idea as a Revolutionary Symbol," *CH*, XXVII (1958); Christopher Hill, *Puritanism and Revolution* (London, 1959); Leo F. Solt, *Saints in Arms* (Stanford, 1959); and Michael Walzer, *The Revolution of the Saints** (Cambridge, Mass., 1965). For further reading on this subject, consult the booklet in this series edited by Philip A. M. Taylor, *The Origins of the English Civil War* (Boston, 1960).

Scores of books have been published about the highly controversial Puritan leader Oliver Cromwell. Among the best are S. R. Gardiner, *Oliver Cromwell* (London, 1899); C. H. Firth, *Oliver Cromwell and the Rule of the Puritans in England* (London, 1901); R. S. Paul, *The Lord Protector* (London, 1955); Maurice Ashley, *Oliver Cromwell and the Puritan Revolution* (London, 1958); Christopher Hill, *Oliver Cromwell*, (London, 1958); and Peter Young, *Oliver Cromwell* (London, 1963). Also of special interest are a pair of books on the political involvement of two other men identified with seventeenth-century English Calvinism: Don Wolfe, *Milton in the Puritan Revolution* (London, 1941) and Richard Schlatter, *Richard Baxter and Puritan Politics* (New Brunswick, N. J., 1961). Anyone interested in more detailed suggestions for further reading on Cromwell and his associates should see the booklet in this series edited by Richard E. Boyer, *Oliver Cromwell and the Puritan Revolt* (Boston, 1966).

A great deal has been written about the relationship between Calvinism and the Glorious Revolution of 1688. Harold J. Laski's *Political Thought in England from Locke to Bentham* (London, 1955) covers the political theory of the revolutionary period. John Stoughton's *The Church of the Revolution* (vol. V of the "History of Religion in England" series, London, 1961) is the most comprehensive church history of the period but should be consulted in conjunction with Charles Mullett's valuable and interesting article entitled "Religion, Politics, and Oaths in the Glorious Revolution," *Review of Politics*, X (1948). John Locke, the key figure in the controversy over the real nature of the connections between Calvinist thought and the revolutionary ideology of 1688, has been the subject of numerous biographies and studies of political theory. Among the best works on Locke and his political thought are: Maurice Cranston, *John Locke: A Biography* (New York, 1957); John Gough, *John Locke's Political Philosophy* (Oxford, 1950); Peter Laslett, "The English Revolution and Locke's 'Two Treatises of Government,'" *Cambridge Historical Journal*, XII (1956); and, brilliantly argued and extremely valuable for an understanding of the Calvinist antecedents of Locke's political ideas, John Dunn, *The Political Thought of John Locke: An Historical Account of the Argument of the 'Two Treatises of Government'* (New York, 1969). For a further discussion of the meaning of the Glorious Revolution, see the booklet in this series on the subject edited by Gerald M. Straka, *The Revolution of 1688* (Boston, 1963).

The following works will provide an adequate introduction to the religious and political currents of the Reformation era in Scotland: John Knox, *History of the Reformation in Scotland*, in *The Works of John Knox*, Daniel Laing, ed. 6 vols. (Edinburgh, 1895); J. M. Reid, *Kirk and Nation*, (London, 1960); A. M. Renwick, *The Story of the Scottish Reformation* (London, 1960); Gordon Donaldson, *The Scottish Reformation* (Cambridge, 1960); J. H. S. Burleigh, *The Church History of Scotland* (London, 1961); and J. D. Douglas, *Light in the North* (Grand Rapids, 1964).

The place of John Knox in the Scottish Reformation and his political thought and influence have been discussed by P. Hume Brown, *John Knox* (New York, 1905); Eustace Percy, *John Knox*, rev. ed. (London, 1965); Jasper Ridley, *John Knox* (Oxford, 1968), an excellent new biography; and J. R. Gray, "The Political Theory of John Knox," *CH*, VII (1939). Of related interest is P. Hume Brown's *George Buchanan, Humanist and Reformer* (Edinburgh, 1890).

EARLY AMERICAN CALVINISM

Two excellent essays demonstrating the connections between Old and New World Puritanism are by Louis B. Wright, *Religion and Empire* (Chapel Hill, 1943) and Alan Simpson, *Puritanism in Old and New England* (Chicago, 1956). Studies which discuss the relationship of colonial American Calvinism to the development of democracy include E. D. Mead, "William Brewster and the Independents," in *Pioneers of Religious Liberty in America*, S. A. Eliot, ed. (Boston, 1903); Perry Miller, *The Puritans* (New York, 1938) and *The New England Mind: the Seventeenth Century* (New York, 1939); R. B. Perry, *Puritanism and Democracy* (New York, 1944); *Foundations of Democracy*, E. E. Johnson, ed. (New York, 1947); A. N. Wilder, "The Puritan Heritage in American Culture," *Theology Today*, V (1948); and Clinton Rossiter, *Seedtime of the Republic* (New York, 1953).

Included among the many useful works on American Calvinist movements and men associated with the growth of Calvinism in the New World are Leonard J. Trinterud, *The Forming of an American Tradition: A Re-examination of Colonial Presbyterianism* (Philadelphia, 1949); M. L. Starkey, *The Congregational Way: The Role of the Pilgrims and Their Heirs in the Shaping of America* (Garland City, N. Y., 1966); S. H. Brockunier, *The Irrepressible Democrat: Roger Williams* (New York, 1940); Mauro Calamandrei, "Neglected Aspects of Roger Williams' Thought," *CH*, XXI (1952); Perry Miller, *Roger Williams: His Contribution to the American Tradition* (New York, 1953); and E. S. Morgan, *The Puritan Dilemma: The Story of John Winthrop* (Boston, 1958).

1 2 3 4 5 6 7 8 9 10